WIN
from
WITHIN

Also by John W. Gray III

I Am Number 8: Overlooked and
Undervalued, but
Not Forgotten by God

WIN *from* WITHIN

FINDING YOURSELF BY FACING YOURSELF

JOHN W. GRAY III

Foreword by Steven Furtick

New York Nashville

FaithWords
Hachette Book Group
1290 Avenue of the Americas, New York, NY 10104
faithwords.com
twitter.com/faithwords

First edition: October 2018

FaithWords is a division of Hachette Book Group, Inc. The FaithWords name and logo are
trademarks of Hachette Book Group, Inc.

The publisher is not responsible for websites (or their content) that are not owned by the
publisher.

The Hachette Speakers Bureau provides a wide range of authors for
speaking events. To find out more, go to www.hachettespeakersbureau.com or
call (866) 376-6591.

Library of Congress Control Number: 2018954706

ISBNs: 978-1-4555-3959-8 (hardcover), 978-1-4555-3957-4 (ebook),
978-1-5460-1085-2 (int'l), 978-1-5460-3552-7 (int'l South African)

Printed in the United States of America

LSC-C

10 9 8 7 6 5 4 3 2 1

For a seed to achieve its greatest expression, it must come completely undone. The shell cracks, its insides come out and everything changes. To someone who doesn't understand growth, it would look like complete destruction.

—Cynthia Occelli

And He said, "Your name shall no longer be called Jacob, but Israel; for you have struggled with God and with men, and have prevailed."

—Genesis 32:28

Contents

Foreword

Different people appreciate different things about John Gray. Some marvel at his ability to break demographic barriers and shift an atmosphere by infusing an entire room with laughter. He's made me laugh until I was out of breath on many occasions, so I understand firsthand how infectious his spontaneous, self-effacing humor can be. But that's not what I appreciate most about him.

Others will cite the depth of insight he brings to the biblical narrative, and his matchless ability to articulate universal truth with the warmth of a personal conversation. I, too, have sat mesmerized as he transported me so fully into a story or principle that I felt like I was hearing the most familiar wisdom for the first time.

And yes, he can sing too. His vocal runs and range make the rest of us wonder if God accidentally unevenly distributed talent on the day John was born.

For most people, this disproportionate mix of gifts, brilliance, and larger-than-life personality would probably be too much to handle. Most people with a fraction of these abilities would probably become the president of their own fan club. Not John. That's what I appreciate most about my friend. Since I've known him, I watched him win over and over again. I've watched doors of influence open to him, and I've watched him limp—not strut—through them.

I've watched him pay the price again and again to win from the only place true victory is possible: within. He fights to maintain a love for people that is never consumed by the size of the crowd. In an age of cliché-infested Christianity, I've seen John demand depth of himself as he wrestles with his own weakness in the shadows of his success. The fact that he has now written about this struggle with his trademark inspiration and vulnerability in tandem is a gift to us all, just as John himself is.

—Steven Furtick, Charlotte, North
Carolina, August 2018

Introduction

What Matters Most

I'm leaving you! I'm packing the kids, getting in the car, and going to my mother's house in Alabama. I won't tell anybody, but I'm not staying!"

With those words, my wife walked out of our home. My life, as I knew it, was over. John Gray, the pastor, the preacher, the traveling evangelist, the guy from TV, the person everybody celebrates, was a private failure. Every principle I'd ever taught came back to haunt me. Every single thing I'd ever believed about myself, relationships, and God walked right out the door behind my wife.

That singular, transformational moment was the result of many moments I'd lived in my forty-four years, moments when I was unable and maybe even unwilling to see the heart of the person I'd promised to love, honor, and protect. So much so that she'd rather go back to the home of her childhood than live another day with me.

To the world, though, I was a magnificent success. I

traveled around the world speaking at all the big Christian conferences. I preached at the largest church in America. And yet, every single day, I was dying on the inside. I was afraid to confront the real issues of my life and ill-equipped to handle the responsibilities of being a husband and father. On top of that, I was unwilling to seek help from those who I knew could be trusted. I allowed the voice of skepticism to convince me that I could protect myself from the blunt force trauma wrought by my choices.

Beyond the sting of my wife's words and the silence that followed, I was left with the reality that what people knew of me was about to change. Everything that I ever said, the monuments of words I built, was going to come crashing down.

And you know what I felt?

Not fear.

Not shame.

Not even guilt.

I felt utter, unequivocal relief.

Finally, the man who had been living two lives in one body would be able to come out from the shadows and declare, "This is me. This is John Gray."

My wife was right. I had abandoned her in the middle of our marriage to nurse, build a monument to, and celebrate me. *She should be glad that I chose her*, I thought.

Something was very wrong with me.

The time for excuses and blame was finally done. I found myself arguing with God. "You're all-knowing and all-powerful. I prayed to you," I would say. "I asked you to deliver me from these habits, from these thoughts, from these things. I asked you to help me and you didn't." I found myself placing blame elsewhere. "I didn't have a father. You were never there and neither was he. Oh, yeah, and my wife? She doesn't understand. She's not a man. She doesn't do what I do."

I was the king of deflection. In my mind, my failures were everyone else's fault. I refused to face anything that would cause me discomfort for very long. If I sensed discomfort, I would change the temperature. If things got too hot, I'd leave. If it got too cold and I felt exposed, I'd layer up. I layered up with comedy. Get someone laughing and you can generally deflect any arrows heading your way.

For a little while, at least.

The worst was when I used my gift to redirect something God wanted to challenge me on. Because I have a gift of discernment, I can always spot when someone else is going through. A classic tactic of mine would be to read someone else's mail before they could dig into mine. That way, whatever they came to tell me would be lost in the reality of their own humanity. In other words, before someone could come sweeping around my front porch, they'd better check their whole house.

In my mind, I set the rules. I set the boundaries. And no matter who you were, if you stepped out of bounds, that very cold part of me that had been fostered over years of being rejected and laughed at in the back of buses on the way to school, that protective casing I created over my emotions and heart, would kick in. I knew how to keep the word of God, the people of God, and even the voice of God out. And I would pat myself on the back for being a survivor. Yeah, I may not be perfect, but look at you. I may not be doing what I need to do, but look over there, look at what he's not doing. That's how gifted men often never heal, grow, or mature. They always have a trick up their sleeves to make people stop challenging them to do exactly those things.

When you're gifted and talented, and your gift has become a commodity, people don't often confront you. Sometimes it's because they need you in some capacity. Other times it's because they are fascinated by or desire you. All of it put me in the worst conundrum. Isolated by my pain, I wanted to be as free as I encourage others to be from the pulpit, but I didn't have the guts to face the root cause of my pain, the root cause of my insecurity. So the life I was living was the life I'd created in a world of my own making. I needed people to tell me the truth, especially when I didn't want to hear it. In fact, I would go as far as to say that if a friend or loved one doesn't make you mad on occasion with their assessment of something you have done, then the relationship is likely not real. If we surround ourselves with yes-men, we risk never becoming everything God wants us to be.

I was headed down that road. I would do anything to not deal with me, and as a result, the woman to whom I promised forever took her forever and walked out the door, taking with her the real legacy of my son and my daughter.

As I was writing this book, my entire life, as I knew it, was over.

And that's exactly what God wanted.

The scariest part of it all is, I was in a "high season." I'd never preached better and never had more opportunities. Every door was opening for me. But the danger of the moment I was in was this: I assumed that because doors were opening for me, God was pleased. It never occurred to me that gifts and callings are truly given without repentance, and we can serve God in one area of our lives and be totally in rebellion and denial in others.

This is how leaders fall.

The pride in our gifts causes us to misinterpret the favor of God. There is a profound difference between God choosing you and God needing you. Something in me mistook God *using* my gifts for God *needing* my gifts. Inasmuch as God is all-powerful and all-knowing, He doesn't need anything. God didn't need me.

But...

God chose to use me as a testament to grace. Sitting in a room alone with the words of my brokenhearted wife pounding against the cavernous, empty space inside of my

unsubmitted heart, I learned that this was the only way
God was ever going to reach me. Success didn't reach me.
Opportunity didn't reach me. So God allowed the only one
who truly saw me for who I was *and stayed anyway*, and
loved me through it, over and over and over again, to be
willing to walk away. The one who'd given me the most
grace was fed up. Only then was I forced to look inside at
the landscape of a man who had everything and nothing.
How did it come to this? How did I become the most successful empty man in ministry? How in the world were so
many people fooled, and if they weren't fooled, then why
didn't they say anything?

For most of us, there is a duality: the desire to be more,
to become more, to achieve more, and to manifest more.
There's a quickening, a stirring, that says this iteration of
me is not the very best me. We can feel it! But too many of
us get stuck and don't go after all that they could be. Or we
buy into false notions of what "winning" looks like and end
up sidetracked from our purpose.

I don't want that for you, and that is why I'm writing
this book.

Inside of this human existence, there is a dynamic
human-divine relational exchange that's not only an opportunity for relational partnership and intimate fellowship
with God, but also an invitation to do something with the

seed of God. To grow! The problem with growth, with becoming great, is that you cannot feel comfortable if you're going to be great. God won't let you. He will stir you. He will shake you. He will prod and push you. It's because He loves you too much to let you die average unless you absolutely choose to.

What I want you to get out of the experience of reading this book is to spot and identify areas where you've stopped moving forward. Look for those places that were supposed to be temporary moments of rest or reflection but which you've made a home. One of the things that happened with Hurricane Katrina was that FEMA came in and created temporary housing, but because of inability, apathy, or the bureaucratic quagmire that often exists as it pertains to social services—or all three—temporary housing became permanent housing. What was supposed to last six months has, for some, lasted until this day. And so it goes with our lives. Some of us are stuck. Some of us are in a moment, much like I was, when everything is falling down around us and it's time for us to move. To do something we've never done before.

My hope is that when you finish reading, you'll say, "Wait a minute! There's some places in my life where I have set up camp and I was never supposed to stay there. Maybe it's time for me to face down the things that are holding me back. Maybe my whole understanding of what it means to win in life is wrong."

*   *   *

Winning doesn't come from things. It doesn't come from obtaining a position or some social status. It doesn't live in the accolades you receive or your achievements. So whether that's being faithful to three hundred, thirty-three thousand, or three million, winning was never about the size of your platform. Winning comes from knowing God and being in His will. It comes from doing what you were created to do in a way that is authentic to your calling.

In my world, it looked like I was winning. I had a big platform—looks like a win. Nice house? Another win. Nice cars? A total win. Married with kids? Yep, looks like a win. Scan all the pictures we post on social media and they certainly look like wins. But those were all one-dimensional images masking the three-dimensional reality that I was empty. I had become hollow because I had given everything that I was to everyone else and had not cultivated the necessary places of spiritual nourishment for my soul. My prayer life began lacking tremendously. I found myself going to the word only when I needed to preach or to give something to someone else. In every significant area, I was losing. I was losing emotionally. I was losing relationally and physically. I was losing spiritually because I was not hungering for the word.

One day I looked in the mirror and said, "That's not the man I want to be." It wasn't just a discomfort with my physical self. I was clear that the physical stuff was the final manifestation of my unhappiness. There were way too many times when I'd put up a social media post and then cringe when people responded to the smile and perceived triumph. I knew the truth. They had no clue of the challenges behind that smile. They had no clue of the pain behind it. They had no clue of the tears I cried just minutes before the pic was taken. What I realized when I looked in the mirror was that I could very well breeze through life having done nice things but nothing great. I would end up being a very low-voltage, low-capacity version of who I'm called to be.

But God wasn't done with me yet. And in that way, I learned that true winning also looks like losing. That's the gist of this book and why Jacob's story is integral to mine and maybe even to yours. See, God used—and is still using—all those broken areas in my life to awaken me, to teach me that my appetites need to change as more responsibility comes. It is an uncomfortable place to realize that you have been gifted with everything you ever wanted just so God could show you that it's nothing that you ever needed.

God is saying to us all that none of those superficial wins I just mentioned can be our end goal. We must be willing to lose it all in order to truly win. Winning from within is about facing ourselves, our deficits, and understanding that true victory happens at the spiritual level.

What is at the root of the losses, the deficits in your life?

I've outlined some of mine here. My marriage suffered. My children suffered. I thought I was only supposed to be the provider. I would come in and out of town from serving the people but couldn't muster the energy and strength to help my kids with their projects in kindergarten. I was so "on fire" for God but I had no energy for my first ministry— my wife, children, and even my own health. These were what mattered most.

The physical, emotional, spiritual, and relational areas of our lives that might be in total disarray are often the same pathways God will use for our self-discovery. I wish there was an easier way to become a man or woman, but there is not.

This is why I identify with Jacob and why he is very much a thread in this book. Jacob was the twin brother of Esau in the womb. From the womb, he wanted to be first, but he was always coming up second. He was always losing.

When you watch football or other sports on TV, no one ever says, "We're number two!" Everybody says, "We're number one." Well, Jacob was perpetually the second guy. He was always coming up short. Esau came out of the womb with Jacob grabbing his heel, and so Jacob's name means supplanter, or heel grabber. Scripture reveals him always grabbing for something he wanted, trying to be something other than what he was. I imagine he was never comfortable in his own skin.

But here's the thing: in all his grabbing, Jacob lacked the aggression and physical form to take over. Esau was the hunter. Esau was the alpha male. His father loved him. Isaac was like, "That's my dude. He's hairy. He kills things. That's my boy!" And Jacob, well, he became the one his mama took to. In an ancient, patriarchal Middle Eastern culture, I can't imagine that your manhood is celebrated when you're in the house cooking with your mama. You're over there doing dishes while your brother's outside with his homies? They're doing archery and bow hunting and you're like, "No, mama, I'll just stay with you."

So I think Jacob represents for so many of us this longing to be something other than what we are. And this wasn't entirely bad in and of itself. There was something in him that knew he was created for more but didn't know how to manifest it. He didn't know that "grabbing" wasn't always the way to win. So everything in Jacob's life revealed his duality. He had a high work ethic but there were times when he lacked integrity in the way he did things. Whew, doesn't that sound familiar? How many of us will trade a little bit of this to get to that? Jacob is a picture of this trade-off: "What do I have to do to get where I want to go?" He would manipulate things in his favor. He was sneaky. He was tricky. He was dishonest.

Whether we want to admit it or not, there are times when all of us have made certain emotional or spiritual or moral trades in order to win, in order to get certain things we want. But in doing so, we trade the truth of who we are for the illusion of who people want us to be. So, like me, Jacob was always two people, and he spent the early part of his life running away from who God was shaping him to be.

But isn't it just like God to say to you, me, and Jacob: "I chose you. You're exactly whom I chose. I knew everything about you and I still chose you. I know all your character flaws, and I still chose you. I know all the places where you lack the necessities of who you believe you're called to be, but if you will face yourself, you will get the key to the final you. The you that is established. The foundational you from where I will begin to establish legacy."

Jacob wrestled with God. The Scripture says, "A man wrestled with him" (Gen. 32:24), and it's in that kind of wrestling, that engagement with God, where we *become*. It's in that place where we awaken. It's in that place where we ignite our passion and our potential.

But the angel of the Lord said, "What is your name?" What the angel was saying is, "Who do you think you are?" He said, finally, "I am Jacob." In other words, "I am the supplanter. I am the trickster. I'm the inauthentic one. I'm the mask wearer. I'm the con artist." Then the angel said, "No, your name will no longer be Jacob but Israel for you had contended with God and with man and have prevailed. You win" (see Gen. 32:28).

What does it mean when somebody says, "That's John Gray"? What will it mean after I'm long gone? Will that name be marked by my bad decisions? Will it be marked by my worst moments? Or will it be marked by the truth of who I was as I was becoming? I hope it's the latter. I think for every human being, that's what we want. I don't mind the places of my failure. I do mind if it's the only thing I'm known for. I want to be more. I want to be known for more than just the things that I did not do properly or correctly, the hurt I caused. I don't mind the work, because it's necessary for the texture of the full portrait to emerge. This work is necessary to win.

Jacob didn't win in his life by his own hand. It wasn't his doing. The journey for Jacob required both personal responsibility and, even more significantly, a supernatural touch. Jacob won because his whole life was a search to find out who he really was. Jacob found himself by facing himself, and in acknowledging his past, the totality of his journey, God announced who he *really* was and who he would be remembered as. In that moment, he had victory. The goal of this book is to help readers begin the process of discovering who they really are in Christ. Knowing who we are is the fuel for knowing what to do with the rest of our lives.

This is what winners are made of. You cannot win until you lose it all. In my case, I had to look into the darkest places of my soul and say, "God, this isn't You. This was never You. This doesn't look like Your word, and I have treated the woman You gave me with utter contempt. There's nothing about my life that even remotely resembles an authentic relationship with Jesus." But I sure was preaching my heart out. I shouted to the rooftops that Jesus saves, but I never let Him save me. I trusted God for everybody else, but I didn't trust Him with my own pain, my own shame, my own guilt, and my own brokenness. In fact, I could sell you God, but I gave God the side-eye. It's like a man who sells a product that he doesn't use. I was a salesman.

I had become the thing I hated: a professional Christian. I didn't know how to change. I was lost, and I was lost in front of millions of eyes. I was lost on TV shows, in church services and conferences. I was smiling and lost; preaching and lost; broken and lost. I had lost it all. I had lost my wife, my children. Every platform I had was poised to be gone in an instant.

But in that moment, when all was lost, God said, "Now we can begin."

CHAPTER ONE

Mama's Boy

When the man saw that he did not prevail against Jacob, he touched his hip socket, and Jacob's hip was put out of joint as he wrestled with him. Then he said, "Let me go, for the day has broken." But Jacob said, "I will not let you go unless you bless me." And he said to him, "What is your name?" And he said, "Jacob."

—Genesis 32:25–27 ESV

I am Jacob."

It's just one sentence, but it is a profound shift in history. A man states the truth, and God takes that truth, expands that truth, expounds upon that truth, and makes a nation out of a simple statement. He said, "I am Jacob," and God said, "You are Israel." That moment reveals a man and his process. Jacob's pain was interpreted and filtered through the lens of an eternal God who created him for this uncomfortable, necessary, face-to-face encounter, all so that what was in him would emerge. But it could only happen when Jacob was willing to engage God with the truth of himself. God turned that truth into a nation, and that mama's boy who dwelled in tents became the father of a nation whose descendants are as numerous as the grains of sand on the seashore.

Who exactly is Jacob? How is it that this man got to see angels ascending and descending upon a ladder? I suppose you have to start with the prophecy over him.

Isaac prayed hard to GOD for his wife because she was barren. GOD answered his prayer and Rebekah became pregnant. But the children tumbled and kicked inside her so much that she said, "If this is the way it's going to be, why go on living?" She went to GOD to find out what was going on. GOD told her,

Two nations are in your womb,
two peoples butting heads while still in your body.
One people will overpower the other,
and the older will serve the younger.

When her time to give birth came, sure enough, there were twins in her womb. The first came out reddish, as if snugly wrapped in a hairy blanket; they named him Esau (Hairy). His brother followed, his fist clutched tight to Esau's heel; they named him Jacob (Heel). (Genesis 25:21–27 MSG)

When Rebekah was pregnant, the word of God said two nations were in her womb, and the older shall serve the younger. This was a prophetic declaration made long before Jacob ever grabbed his brother's heel and pushed his way onto this plane. This is important to understand as we look at the context of the life of Jacob. It's easy for us, especially me as a preacher and pastor, to interpret Jacob's life solely through the lens of him being a supplanter, trickster, and heel grabber. He was certainly all of those things. He absolutely had character issues. But he was also chosen by God despite these things. For some, this is evidence of a kind of divine election, and for others it reflects God's understanding of the depth of Esau's failings.

So was there some flaw in Esau that ultimately would have been greater than anything that Jacob could do? Was his heart that problematic? Or was this God simply choosing Jacob regardless? I'm inclined to believe the former but I'm not sure I can break this down either way. At the end of the day, here's what this story indicates for me: Jacob was the beneficiary of a great prophecy before he was even born. His purpose was greater than any negative thing attached to his name. We should all take note: We are all God's creation. We all have a purpose that existed long before any of our flaws did. And that purpose will outlast us.

You see, Jacob has been dead for thousands of years. The texts by which we learn of him are also a few thousand years old. And yet here I am, writing about him. Referencing him. Applying his life to my own. How does that happen?

In short, God talked about him. When God speaks you into being, you cease being just an idea. God's word created the universe, so His word about you has the power to make you eternal. You become something that cannot be ignored. But not only is your purpose particular to you; so is the journey you must walk to get there.

Mama's Boy

I alluded to this earlier, but Jacob was a mama's boy, a mama's boy living in the house with his father. In our modern context, we often associate mama's boys with young men who don't have their dad around. Or, if their dad is around, they don't live in the same house. This is a little different. It was clear from Scripture that Isaac loved Esau. Genesis 25:28 says, "Isaac, who had a taste for wild game, loved Esau, but Rebekah loved Jacob." Esau was the hairy one who would kill things and make great food. Jacob dwelled among the tents. He was a homebody. Esau was, according to all the criteria of the time, a man's man, and Jacob was soft. I imagine Isaac thought, *Yeah, you're my son, Jacob, but Esau is the preferred one.*

In the culture and climate from which Jacob emerged, it's clear that the firstborn was favored. The firstborn was usually the one who received the inheritance from the father. The firstborn usually held all the rights and the authority related to the estate of the family. That is, unless there's an intervention by God, as there was in this case. Nevertheless, both the biblical and historical precedent are clear: Isaac loved Esau, but Rebekah loved Jacob.

Which is weird, because you don't usually expect a mother to play favorites. Especially when they have sons. Especially in that culture. The firstborn that breaks the womb is consecrated to God. This is major. And yet Rebekah was like, "Yo, I just love Jacob." For most of us, when raising children, we love them equally. When a mother births a child—a son or daughter—under what circumstances would you cease to love them? None. Yet that's not necessarily what we see here.

Allow me a little room here for speculation. I think Rebekah might have seen that Jacob was not being embraced by his father. Isaac might have been saying, "Esau is the firstborn. He gets the double portion. I need to invest here." But Rebekah held on to the prophecy. Rebekah held on to the word about her little boy. She responded to Jacob according to the word.

Not unlike another mama's boy—this one from Cincinnati, Ohio, and not ancient Canaan.

There was never a point in my youth when I was not with my mother. No matter what my mother was doing, she kept me close. When she was going to college at night, she would pick me up at the after-school program after work and we would go to Redding Road to eat. Then we would drive to where she was having class. I would sit in this little open area while she went to class, and I knew not to act up. I knew not to be loud. I barely moved but I was there. When we were at church, or if she had rehearsal, I was there also. Even if I wasn't singing, I was there. My mother made sure that at every juncture—no matter what might have been going on— I knew I was not an afterthought. I was constantly in her thoughts. I was constantly a part of the fabric of the decisions that she made. That's what happens when you love someone.

So I don't think we can write off Jacob as *just* a mama's boy—with all the negative connotations that come with that—without some careful thought of the positive impact of that. Rebekah loved Jacob. And while we can debate all day as to whether she should have *preferred* him (or Isaac, Esau), I think the key thing to remember is that because of her love, she saw Jacob. It's likely that she hurt for him, as she knew that Jacob might have longed for a more meaningful relationship with Isaac.

I get this.

The truth is, my mother was all I had. I didn't have anyone else. I didn't have the luxury of a father speaking into me. He wasn't around, but my mother was, and she invested in me. Everything that I am is because she invested it or prayed it. If I ever have impact beyond my life span, it will be because my mother loved me.

The Drawbacks

All this said, identifying as a mama's boy doesn't make you weak but it does have some drawbacks. It did for Jacob and it certainly did for me. The connection between a mother and child is natural. In most cases, moms are the first to nurture and care for the child, feeding him or her from her own breast. But what is initially a perfectly natural bonding experience—a significant connection for growth—can turn into codependence. And that codependence could negatively impact the development of a son into a man.

One place where I wish my mother had maybe prepared me a little better is for the aggression and toxicity that can come from masculinity. Growing up as a tween and teen in the late '70s, early '80s, there were moments where you had to fight. It just happened. Dudes on the playground were taking in the pop culture around them and being aggressive. There was this instinctual, animalistic, posturing thing going on. *Who's the strongest in the crew? Who's the weakest?* I remember being in my home and telling my mom that these guys were pushing and bullying me, and she told me not to fight. I'll never forget what she said: "I never want you to fight unless you are absolutely in a corner and cannot get away. Do not fight. The only time you have permission to fight is if you are physically backed into a corner and cannot get away." And I took that to heart.

The problem is, very rarely are you actually in a physical corner in a fight. So I became the guy that would encounter these aggressions and would not defend myself. I'd walk away or I would figure out some other way to get out. Without any explanation of why it's not good to fight or why defending myself might be necessary in more instances than being in a corner, it messed with me. I constantly thought, *Am I weak?* I had no construct for knowing what was strength or weakness. So in my young mind, I bought the lie that I was weak because I wasn't aggressive. Which led to, I was uncool because we didn't have cable or a VCR growing up, so I didn't know all the current lingo. Which led to all the other ways I felt less than, and ultimately to insecurity.

In one way, being a mama's boy was great because I knew that my mother would protect me. She loved and provided for me. But the drawback was the insecurities that came when I didn't have a clear understanding of my identity as a man or my manhood. Being a mama's boy leaves you open to seeing yourself as weaker or less than, when in fact you're just *different from.* My life was evidence of this and clearly, so was Jacob's. The dynamic between Esau and Jacob was a "greater and less-than" situation from the beginning. Remember the prophecy?

And the Lord told her, "The sons in your womb will become two nations. From the very beginning, the two nations will be rivals. One nation will be stronger than the other; and your older son will serve your younger son." (Genesis 25:23 NLT)

The one who was supposed to have the double portion was actually going to end up serving the one who shouldn't have the inheritance. But what happens in the duration?

What happens before the prophecy comes true? For Jacob, for me, and maybe even for you, a lot of *less-than* thinking. For the longest time, I had a *less-than* mentality. I don't know that I would call it a loser's mentality, but it was a less-than mentality. When we would play sports on the playground after school, I would be picked last, and that's just what it was. I knew I was going to be picked last, because I wasn't athletic and my working mother who grew up during a certain era didn't cultivate that in me.

These kinds of events in our lives, things that reinforce the less-than mentality, can mess with our psyches. It's easy to lose sight of your purpose, the word God has spoken over you, when you are in certain environments that make you feel less than. It's hard to see the win down the road when you're constantly losing. And so, all too often, we'll start manipulating situations in order to figure out ways to ascribe value to ourselves because, like Jacob and Esau, the natural order of things has put us in a position deficit—and it seems like all the mama's love in the world can't make it right. And yet, our inheritances still seek us out.

Your Inheritance Is Looking for You

I know that the idea of an inheritance seeking you out sounds strange, especially in light of our exploration of Jacob and his manipulations to obtain an inheritance. But that's exactly why it's important to understand. See, despite

what people said about him, or even any "less-than" thinking he might have had, the word from the Lord that was
spoken when Isaac and Rebekah gave birth to Jacob and
Esau still remained. No matter what happened between that
prophecy and the moment Jacob became Israel, God still
pursued Jacob with promise in hand. Yes, He disciplined
him. Yes, Jacob had to go through a process of refining his
character. We'll dig into all of that. But the inheritance was
his and it sought him out.

Allow me to maybe make this more clear: Two years
ago, I got a phone call when my wife and I were still living
in Atlanta. The person on the other end of the phone asked
for "John W. Gray III." My whole name. So you know what
I thought, right? I was prepared with my "I have no money,
Bill Collector" response. The person on the other end of
the phone said, "No, we actually have an inheritance for
you because your grandfather was working on a top-secret
government project."

I was stunned.

My grandfather passed when I was two years old of a
certain, very specific, and rare type of cancer. It was likely
because of the materials he was working with on the job. The
person went on to share how they'd been actively looking for
his heir, and because my mother had kept her married name
even after the divorce, they were able to find her, then me.
They said, "Because of what your grandfather did, we have a
check for you."

Because of what my grandfather did.

I didn't earn that check. I didn't know it was coming. But it was mine.

My inheritance was looking for me.

The Role of the Family in Identity

The earliest definition of who we are usually comes from the people who influenced us. More clearly, from those who raised us. Very rarely does a person graduate beyond what's been declared over them—particularly from the primary caregiver, the parental structure, whether it's the actual birth parents, adoptive parents, or extended family. Sometimes those dynamics can be healthy, and other times not so much. I think every parent who has some modicum of stability in their mental makeup believes that their child is the best thing that's ever lived, and they want to see them do well. But there are also other factors that play a part in parents putting their children in unhealthy predicaments and teaching them bad habits.

Now Rebekah was listening when Isaac spoke to his son Esau. So when Esau went to the field to hunt for game and bring it, Rebekah said to her son Jacob, "I heard your father speak to your brother Esau, 'Bring me game and prepare for me delicious food, that I may eat it and bless you before the LORD before I die.' Now therefore, my son, obey my voice as I command you. Go to the flock and bring me two good young goats, so that I may prepare from them delicious food for your father, such as he loves. And you shall bring it to your father to eat, so that he may bless you before he dies." But Jacob said to Rebekah his mother, "Behold, my brother Esau is a hairy man, and I am a smooth man. Perhaps my father will feel me, and I shall seem to be mocking him and bring a curse upon myself and not a blessing." His mother said to him, "Let your curse be on me, my son; only obey my voice, and go, bring them to me." (Genesis 27:5–13 ESV)

If you look at Rebekah and Jacob, you see that while she loved Jacob, she also, in many ways, taught him how to be sneaky. How to connive. The family dynamics were not healthy, and a segment of Jacob's questionable moral compass could have been a direct reflection of the emotional absence of his father and the overcompensation of his mother.

Even though I did not see myself in any particular way—good or bad—my mother always seemed to have what I thought were rose-colored glasses when it came to me. At first, I thought it was because I was an only child. When I look at the dynamics of my family—my mother and her siblings especially—she's really unique. She stands out from her seven brothers and sisters in that she really embraced the principles of Christ fellowship and discipleship and implemented the word, study, and prayer, living it out on a daily basis. Her life was so extraordinary that I'm actually living in the residue of it.

I have not yet invested the time that my mother has in her relationship with God, but I'm a beneficiary of it because she spoke to me as if she knew something I did not know. And when you hear over and over again a particular thing, you begin to believe it even if you don't see it. That thing can be negative, as in the case of Jacob and Rebekah, or positive, as in the case of my mother. I think many of us are shaped by the words of people who have been given authority and power over us.

Family dynamics are significant. For example, one of my uncles was developmentally disabled. Still another battled mental illness and was on government assistance. The men in my family were not anything to emulate. So, in terms of how I would need to define myself, being a mama's boy was the only chance I had of breaking that cycle. If I was going to become like the men in my family, then addiction and bad decisions and all types of other vices would've been my life. It's very clearly in my bloodline, and it's in my DNA. And yet there are things I've done, stuff that's manifested, that I would not possibly have been able to do without my mother's influence. Family dynamics and their influence is not just about nature or just about nurture. It's not binary. There are some things that are nurtured and there are some things that are innate.

Jacob didn't manipulate because he was wicked. He

manipulated, he connived, because he was influenced by the family dysfunction. But it's not all on Rebekah either. Jacob stole the birthright because he wanted more. The truth is, most of us wrestle with our actual identities and manipulate our way to the one we think we want, because we just want more.

More and More and More

The word *more* is linguistically small, but it's huge when we consider its various meanings. It's a broad word and it can mean anything to anybody at any time. When we aren't strong and secure in who we are or in what we're purposed to do, we tend to want more than what's allotted to us. Big more. Which is different from wanting more of a specific, tangible thing. Little mores. There are lots of people who want the proverbial more. Big more. Not necessarily more money or clothes. Those are little mores. Wanting more money is usually about wanting more freedom. See? That's a little more vs. a big more. Wanting more money is really about being able to breathe and not worry about having to pay bills or if there will be money in the account for food.

I've been in seasons of wanting more. To the casual observer, saying this might sound or look selfish, self-centered, or ungrateful, because I have a nice house; I've got nice vehicles; I'm at a big church. And yet the evidence of my needing to find my big more was when I realized that, despite all those things, I was profoundly unhappy. There is a not a house, car, or church building on the planet that can satisfy the longing in the soul.

I don't want to be well known. I want to matter. I want what I do to matter. And that's where I think I identify with Jacob's "grab" for significance. As manipulative and wrong as it was to steal his brother's birthright, it's entirely possible that Jacob believed himself to be drifting into a very certain anonymity. He was a mama's boy, not a great hunter. He was second born, not first. These things must have weighed on him. I've always said that the only thing worse than dying is being forgotten.

"You ever heard of John Gray?"

"Who? Nah. What'd he do? Who was he?"

I don't want that. I want people to say, "Oh yeah, John Gray lived and he did something great." But here's the catch: Greatness is not defined by the magnitude of one's platform or the number of eyeballs on you. Greatness has nothing to do with status or the level of applause you receive. Greatness is defined by functioning in and meeting the threshold of what is acceptable and pleasing to God in your life.

All I've ever wanted was for God to be pleased with me. It's the only reason He's still using me with all my flaws and screwups. So much of what has happened in my life has been so atypical that, if I'm honest, there are many, many nights I dream of going back to Cincinnati, finding work, getting a little apartment for my family, and singing at the local church. That dream, I think, is about drifting into invisibility because, by man's account, there is absolutely no reason why God should use me—except that I love Him and I only want Him to be pleased.

Thousands of years apart, Jacob and John both came to the moment of awareness and discovery. Maybe this is where you are too. In order to establish an eternal legacy, Jacob had to stop running and face himself. John Gray also had to stop running and face himself. And *you* must stop running and face yourself. Everything that Jacob believed in was on the other side. If he turned back, he was going to have to face Esau, and if he went forward, he was going to have to encounter God. Either way, he was going to have to wrestle. Who he chose to wrestle and who he chose to engage is why we're talking about him now. That's the lesson. Whether you are a mama's boy or a daddy's girl or neither, if you only engage the people from your past or the things from your past, then that gives you only one access point. But when we engage God, He can give us an understanding of where we came from in a way that no one else can.

The difference between Jacob wrestling Esau and Jacob wrestling with God is that, with the former, he would've only been battling with the demons of his childhood. Jacob was seeking his blessing the right way this time. Instead of wrestling to obtain an earthly blessing, he was wrestling God for God. Because God, in that moment, was all he wanted. God was the only one who could heal and change his heart. There was so much more at stake.

When Jacob wrestled God, he was actually battling the better angel of his future—the thing that was promised, the thing that was prophesied, the *more* that he so desperately wanted. We are all in a battle between our flesh and our spirit; between our history and our calling; between our nature and the prophetic word that's been slowly nurtured over us by an oh-so-patient God.

CHAPTER TWO

Where Is Your Altar?

> And he came to a certain place and stayed there that night, because the sun had set. Taking one of the stones of the place, he put it under his head and lay down in that place to sleep. And he dreamed.
>
> —Genesis 28: 11–12 ESV

In God's economy the only way that you're going to be victorious, the only way to win, is by putting Him first. And sometimes putting God first looks like laying down and losing—until you look a little closer.

In Genesis 28, Jacob has left his mother and father's house. He'd stolen Esau's birthright and was now running from his brother. He goes to sleep one night in what the Bible calls *a certain place*. Not random, but particular. It was night. He gets a rock. He lays on the rock, and he goes to sleep. Jacob has a lot on his mind. He is a fugitive. His brother is searching for him to kill him. His mother has told him to leave everything he knows. His life is on the line. His father is really nowhere to be found. Jacob is alone, scared, and he is exhausted.

Jacob isn't alone though. We have all sat in the "certain place." Think about the moment when everything changed for you. Maybe that moment is now. When the weariness of your life—how you might have lived it thus far and the results of that living—catches up to you, you realize that you can no longer move forward without a change. That's when you know you've reached your own "certain place," when you know that who you are isn't who you were created to be.

What a man does when he is weary reveals the substance of who he is. When we are weary, we are prone to sin, at worst, or to make unwise decisions, at the least. But I would argue that Jacob wasn't just weary from his physical journey. He was also exhausted from the emotional toll of his perceived identity. He saw himself as always being second; always trying to catch up; always trying to fit in. He was the earliest incarnation of the mama's boy in a patriarchal society. And now he comes to this desert, and he uses a rock as a pillow. It might be cliché to say, but Jacob was literally caught between a rock and a hard place: the stone on which he slept and the hard place of wanting meaning to his life. Jacob needed direction and clarity of purpose.

The rock and the hard place is where too many of us give up. We don't wait for the dream to come. As we see in verse 12, God showed up for Jacob. He showed in a dream. And in this dream, God prophesies and declares what His intent, heart, and mind are toward Jacob. What Jacob does next is another model for winning.

Worship and Enlightenment

When Jacob awakens, he is stunned by the realization that he'd just visited a place that is the conduit between earth and heaven. He was in a supernatural physical location, and his mind had been the doorway to the supernatural realm of the spirit. So he takes oil and he pours it all over the rock he was laying on.

> So early in the morning Jacob took the stone that he had put under his head and set it up for a pillar and poured oil on the top of it. He called the name of that place Bethel, but the name of the city was Luz at the first. Then Jacob made a vow, saying, "If God will be with me and will keep me in this way that I go, and will give me bread to eat and clothing to wear, so that I come again to my father's house in peace, then the LORD shall be my God, and this stone, which I have set up for a pillar, shall be God's house." (Genesis 28:18–22 ESV)

So the very stone that Jacob was laying on became the place where he worshiped. The place where he laid his head in pure exhaustion was now the place where he bowed his knee. That stone went from a place of rest and dreaming to a place of worship and awareness.

Where is the place where you meet and dwell with God? Where is your home base? For Jacob, it was Bethel (loosely translated as House of God). He said, "Surely, the Lord lives here. Truly, this is where the Lord dwells and I didn't know it" (see Gen. 28:16). Jacob realized he was in a sacred place, and if we're going to find longtime victory in our lives, we are also going to have to identify our Bethel—the place where we meet with God. This is the place where there are no distractions. A place where we can take the cares of our life—like Jacob—and bring them to God. A place where God will reveal the heavens to us.

And guess what? The Bible doesn't say that Jacob was praying when he laid his head on the stone. It doesn't even say he was worshiping. It just says he was in position. It's easy to fall into the trap of trying to impress God with our churchy words and phrases. We try to please Him with our colloquialisms, our witty, pithy one-liners. God's not interested in any of that. What He's really interested in is a weary heart. Psalm 51: 17 says, "My sacrifice, O God, is a broken spirit: a broken and contrite heart you, God, will not despise." So when God sees that you are at the end of your rope, and you really don't have anywhere else to go, and you're searching for truth, He'll come and meet you.

Build your altar at the place where God showed up for you.

Jacob probably didn't even know how to articulate where he was as a man. He built an altar *after* the fact—after his encounter with God. This is important because so many of us think we have to have a level of spiritual maturity before God will show up. We think we must have some deep revelation, and then God will appear like, "Oh, good. You found me." That's not the case. You don't have to know the words. Your heart can be broken in a million little pieces and God will come talk to you. Him speaking to you validates what He's placed in you. Him speaking to you, dining with you, and overall engaging with you, is proof that His hand is on you.

Jacob's response to God gives us some really great insight to glean from. His gut, instinctual reaction to this vision he had was to build an altar. He said, "God was here, and I didn't know it." And how many times have we walked through moments in life, looked back, and said, "God was there. I didn't know it." God's love and grace are so heavy here. He allows us enough time to get it right. When we can identify places where He showed up—that's how we grow spiritually. It's how we mature. It's how we identify the purposes and plans of God. It's how we win.

Again, I ask, Where is your altar? Where is the place you meet with God? Jacob had Bethel. Later on, many years later, Samuel had Ramah (see 1 Sam. 8:4). Samuel judged Israel on a circuit, but he always returned to Ramah because that was where he built an altar to the Lord.

Building an altar to the Lord means you're establishing spiritual roots. As any gardener knows, the health of the roots of a plant very often determines the quality of its fruit. There are too many times when we seek sustenance outside ourselves. We think likes and shares on Facebook and Instagram will fill us, and for a while, the validation is satisfying. Until it's not. We build altars on unstable ground and then find ourselves wondering why we feel anxious and out of sorts so much. It's because we aren't building an altar on fertile ground, a place where roots can be nourished, where our souls can receive the kind of food that will sustain our God-ordained legacies.

But the altar is a place where your family can gather. It's a place of priority. It's the place where you demonstrate the prioritization of God's presence over God's provision. When you establish an altar, you're saying, "I don't have to get anything from You, God, because You are enough. If I have You, then I have enough. Receiving things from Your hands is secondary to receiving a word from Your heart or word from Your mouth." I'd rather hear God speak, and know that He is directing me, than get something from His hands. Sure, I'm grateful for whatever He gives me, but I'd rather have the interaction and the intimacy of dialogue with Him.

Jacob didn't sense God. He heard God. God spoke to him. And He spoke to him not when all was well. He spoke to him when Jacob was overrun with weariness and in trouble. He had a troubled heart and mind. This should give all of us comfort.

God is not waiting for us to get into some Zen state. We don't have to "clear our minds and think of nothing." God offers us peace. The kind that passes all understanding. The kind that guards our hearts and minds. So despite the many troubles and cares, God shows up. And when He does, we should build an altar and return to that place as often as we can.

The Humbling Place

God knows where you are. He knows what He placed in you. He might even have shown you what He has in store for you. But do you have an altar yet? Where is your stopping point? As I noted earlier, that rock where you rest your head is really a reflection of your priorities. What are your priorities? Is your priority to please people or God? Is your priority simply to achieve academically or professionally, or is your goal to become spiritually mature and complete so that you can be effective for the building of God's kingdom? In all of that, your rock represents where your priorities come under submission. It is your humbling place. James 4:10 says, "Humble yourselves therefore before the Lord, and He shall lift you up." For every believer, there is a requisite level of humility that must accompany your calling. In fact, a lack of relationship skills often reveals itself in our lack of humility and unwillingness to forgive.

None of us deserve to be in the presence of God, but He receives us, and our brokenness, just the same.

Some of us don't know what true humility is. We think of it as solely a kind of disregard of self. We view people who are humble as having a lack of self-awareness. That's not true. Humility doesn't require us to deny what God has placed in us. It just requires us to have some perspective, to be clear that the power through which our gifts function is from God and God alone. We didn't deserve it. We didn't earn it. It was given to us so that we can accomplish the purpose of our lives, and God will make us acutely aware of His power in order to help us arrive at that purpose.

You haven't been called by God if you haven't been broken by God. It took Jacob coming to his broken place for God to say, "Now I can start speaking to him. I can begin to put the pieces together. I can show him some stuff."

At this point, it can be very easy to get legalistic in your expression and approach to God. Religious legalism is about repetition. Don't show up at your "altar" every third Thursday at 2:36 p.m. and demand God's presence. That's not how any of this works! God does not dwell inside religious ceremonies exclusively. God is relational, and so what Jacob shows us is a relational exchange. A heavenly father saw a son who was troubled and in trouble, and He met him in his pain. God met Jacob in his questions. Dare I say, in his doubt? The Bible doesn't say that Jacob asked for direction. It doesn't say he asked for clarity. As far as we can tell, he didn't ask for anything. He just set up the rock and lay down. What a beautiful picture of humility, of surrender. We say, "Lord, I don't know where I am. I don't know what to do. I'm gonna just lay down." And God says, "Let Me tell you what I have planned for you." God sent that word so Jacob wouldn't give up.

What Jacob (and All of Us) Need

The altar is not for God. God doesn't need altars from men. We create and erect altars to God to remind ourselves that we are not alone and that we are participating in a plan that both predates and outlasts us. The altar is about perspective. Life didn't start with you, and it won't end with you. We all play our role. We all play our position. And ultimately, we trust the Lord to get us where He wants us to be.

> Now unto him that is able to keep you from falling, and to present you faultless before the presence of his glory with exceeding joy, To the only wise God our Saviour, be glory and majesty, dominion and power, both now and ever. Amen. (Jude 24–25 KJV)

For me, this is incredibly profound. God met with a very unscrupulous man who had just stolen the birthright from his brother and was a fugitive from his own house. Jacob had no place to go, but God meets with him in the desert and tells him his future. So he builds an altar to elevate that moment and say, "God met me right here. It was a desert, but I'm going to turn it into a house. I'm going to house my worship. I am going to encapsulate it. I'm going to erect a place of celebration, of honor, of remembrance, because God met me right here."

Whew!

The practical application of this is in Jacob's willingness to lay down and his willingness to worship. When and how do we prioritize the presence of God over the cares of life? Can God speak to us? Can He reach us? Or do we say, "Hold on, God, for a second. Let me check on my kids." Or, "Hold on for a second, I need to check my latest social media numbers." Is there any place in our lives where we can be totally devoted to God? Because when we create those spaces where we can lay life down, God responds. By laying it all down, we essentially are saying, "Hey, God. You can speak with me at Your leisure, without interruption. I am available to You. Speak. Give me direction. Give me wisdom. Give me guidance."

What does this have to do with winning from within? Well, the altar is where the old you starts to die, in order that the you that God has called can emerge and live. Jacob was weary. He was ready to give up. But he knew enough to lay down on that hard place. And so God Himself prophesied to Jacob. God spoke to him and gave Jacob something to look forward to. And Jacob built an altar so he would never forget.

My Personal Altar

I don't want you to think that because I'm writing this book that somehow I've mastered all this. I haven't. I need the Lord, and I'm desperate for Him. Much like Jacob, I've had my own encounters with God, experiences where I've had to build an altar to remind myself what God has said. I'm usually able to find my "laying down" place in the rare silence of my home. Sometimes I build my altar to God while sitting in my back window, looking at the trees and searching the skies. I love to sit still, but I don't often get a chance to do that. That's where the whole idea of our rock being a reflection of our priorities can get complicated for so many of us.

I have two small children and an extremely busy life. My wife has needs. There are times when the busyness of my life as an evangelist has choked away at the things that actually should be my top priority. But there is no excuse. Just like Jacob, just like you, I must find the time and space to meet with God. In this season, my altar might be in one place for a particular time, and then, when I get silenced and quiet again, I'll make another somewhere else.

This is why I said we cannot turn our altar building, our meeting with God, into a legalistic endeavor. You don't have to feel like you are stuck having only one altar. This is the worst of what we have begotten in religion. Too many of us are taught to say, "I'm going to only meet with God at

6:08 a.m. every day." Certainly God might honor that and meet us there. Maybe He wants that kind of consistency and discipline from you. But what about the new mom who has to wake up every three hours to feed her newborn? Or what about the student who goes to school full time and works the overnight shift? For them, 6:08 a.m. might not be a feasible time. And yet God wants to meet with them also.

God's not terribly interested in the religious repetition that we associate with meeting with Him. He's so much more than that. The prompting of the Holy Ghost should mark us. If God says, "Hey, come see me at 4:58 a.m." on one day but says "Come spend time with me at twelve noon" the next day, we need to be available.

A Place of Returning

God spoke to Jacob: "Go back to Bethel. Stay there and build an altar to the God who revealed himself to you when you were running for your life from your brother Esau." (Genesis 35:1 MSG)

Later on, Jacob would return to the altar at Bethel, in remembrance (see Gen. 35). The beauty of an altar is, it's not just an initial meeting place. It's also a place of returning. You're always able to come home. You're always able to remember where God met you. It's a place you can take your spouse, your children, and say, "I remember when

God spoke to me here. I remember what He said to me. I remember what I was feeling. I remember my state of mind before God spoke, and now I can tell you what He was doing."

The altar is really about the creation of a safe place to allow God to speak to us. Sure, we can talk to God there, but it really is less about us and more about God initiating the conversation that is necessary for our development. God whispered to Jacob as he lay down, and I believe He is whispering the same to us: *Who you've been is not all that you are, and it is not all that you shall become.*

This is a necessary word that shifts what we think it means to win. God is likely not going to waste these altar calls on getting you that job or some money. Those kinds of things are only by-products of what he wants to do within you first.

CHAPTER THREE

Birthright Gone Wrong

> And let us not be weary in well doing: for in due sea-
> son we shall reap, if we faint not.
>
> —Galatians 6:9 KJV

There is a place past tired. There is a space past sleepy. That's where weariness lives. One of the things we all need to really think about is whether our weariness with life plays a role in our inability to wait on God or operate within his timing.

For Esau, it did.

And Esau said to Jacob, "Let me eat some of that red stew, for I am exhausted!" (Therefore his name was called Edom.) Jacob said, "Sell me your birthright now." Esau said, "I am about to die; of what use is a birthright to me?" Jacob said, "Swear to me now." So he swore to him and sold his birthright to Jacob. Then Jacob gave Esau bread and lentil stew, and he ate and drank and rose and went his way. Thus Esau despised his birthright. (Genesis 25: 30–34 ESV)

Weariness is one of the most diabolical tricks of the enemy. It has caused so many people to fall and fail. Why? Because weariness is rooted in our desire to win. It is an outgrowth of trying to manufacture our own wins as opposed to following God's plan for winning, which doesn't always look the way the culture has defined it for us.

Weariness is actually rooted in a desire to achieve and function at a high level and to ascend to the highest point and produce at the highest capacity. What happens with weariness is you don't just lose strength. You lose liquid. You lose resources. Worst of all, you lose vision. When you're weary, you don't see clearly. When you're weary, you are dehydrated. When you're dehydrated, you'll drink things you don't need in order to quench your thirst.

How Much Is That Stew?

Esau had it all. But because of a temporary hunger, he was willing to give it away. He didn't understand his birthright. When we don't understand spiritual matters, and when we don't understand the power that lies in the order of things, we are too often impulsive enough to, as Esau did, trade our long-term benefits for short-term pleasure or gain. We end up forgoing our birthright, all because of our weariness in the moment. We must persevere. And while we might not clearly understand what we have—which of course is the reason why we often fail in certain areas—we do need to keep our faith in the One who gave "it" to us.

When Esau came in from the field, the Bible says, he was weary. It doesn't say he was tired. It doesn't say he was sleepy. It says he was weary.

As I've said, weary is another level of exhaustion. It's when you're tired in your soul. Things don't make sense and you are willing to risk it all to correct that. You don't care about consequences when you're weary. You might even understand the consequences, but it still doesn't matter.

Weariness is often the accumulation of many moments where you didn't stop to rest, recharge, refresh, and assess. It is often a by-product of constant running, constant doing, and constant working.

But not resting is a setup. It doesn't just cause your stomach to growl, it causes your soul to become hollow, hardened. You don't listen to the voice of the Holy Ghost. You move on to your base instinct. You find yourself moving from appetite to appetite. (More on appetite in a moment.)

I imagine that Jacob had observed his brother. He might have known that Esau was in a state of weariness, and if he was going to strike, if there was ever a moment to get the birthright, this was the time. He didn't just happen to be making a stew. He made it anticipating that Esau would be weary.

Weariness leveled the playing field for Jacob. Jacob didn't have any advantage over Esau. What he had was an uncommon patience, and he waited for Esau to walk in weary. When he walked in weary, his defenses were down and all he was looking for was something to satisfy the hunger.

This principle can be played out in every area of an individual's life. In a marriage, many people get caught up in affairs, whether physical or emotional, not out of curiosity but out of weariness. A soul weariness that leaves you hollow but has an echo.

You don't feel like your needs are being met. You don't feel like you're able to be understood, and so the enemy, who has been watching you sink further into your weary despair, will catch you off guard and cause you to believe that a person you're in covenant with doesn't have what you need. You will seek what you're missing.

I find myself in this particular moment in my life trying to build relational credibility with my wife and my children because, for so long, my life as it was constructed put my wife and children in third and fourth place in my priorities. My "calling" was the most important, I thought. For a long time, I wasn't meeting the emotional, spiritual, and physical needs of my wife and children. My attitude was, *As long as I'm providing, y'all should be fine. I'm serving the Lord over here. Be proud of me.*

But then the truth stared me down when I found myself running ragged all over the world but not leading my family. I woke up weary.

And guess what? The enemy was waiting with stew. The next time you see something that the enemy sends in a moment of weariness, you need to say, "Oh, there goes that stew." I don't care how handsome he is, his name is Stew. I don't care what she looks like, her name is Stew. I don't care what the opportunity is, its name is Stew. Stew is designed to get you to leave the thing God wants to give you. Your purpose and destiny are rightfully yours, and the only way the enemy can get them is if you give them to him. Don't sell your birthright for stew; it's not worth it.

So yes, I admit it: I found myself looking for stew. Out of God's grace, there were many times when God Himself knocked the stew off the table. Even when I was willing to pay the price, He wouldn't let me.

Now unto him that is able to keep you from falling, and to present you faultless before the presence of his glory with exceeding joy, To the only wise God our Saviour, be glory and majesty, dominion and power, both now and ever. Amen. (Jude 24–25 KJV)

Fast if you have to. Drink water if you must. But don't sell your birthright. So many people live a life of regret because they made permanent decisions in a moment of temporary discomfort or hunger.

What the devil never reveals is the lie that whatever we are looking for—the stew he sends our way—will never satisfy the whole of us. Too often we run in the direction of our need and not to the God who supplies all our needs. So when we attempt to fill ourselves with temporal things when we can only be satisfied with spiritual eternal things, we find ourselves in a cycle of weary. A cycle of weary will have you moving from place to place because nothing feels like home. And then you'll run into what I call the great mirage. Your eyes start to play tricks on you and make a thing look better than it is. It's just stew, Esau. You don't even know if it tastes good.

But that didn't matter, right? He saw it. He smelled it. And that was enough.

When we think of any marketplace, there is an uncomfortable truth we must face: a thing costs what a person is willing to pay. Esau had the birthright to pay. He got what he wanted, right?

Well, not exactly.

I've been transparent about the fact that there have been times when my marriage was on the rocks. In those moments, I desired to hear the words of someone other than my wife to affirm me. Here's what I learned: the enemy will always send you what you think you need, he just never tells you how much it costs. He gives it to you first and then he sends you the bill after.

A Legacy in Danger

Weariness has cost many their legacies. In my capacity as a pastor, I've had the privilege of being the confidant of many men who found themselves in some very dark places because they got weary. One leader I hold very dear said this to me regarding my acceptance of a new Senior Pastor position at my church: "John, my concern for you is that as a lead pastor you don't allow space for the enemy to thrive." He went on to say, "I want your marriage to be strong, because if it's not, you will only hear the noise of the cheerleaders, the crowd. You will confide in the wrong one. You will end up making the decisions that I've made."

This person is one of the most brilliant theological minds to have emerged in the last hundred years, and here he was, admitting that he'd been Esau, willing to lose his legacy because of exhaustion. He said, "I was so weary and tired that I actually started dating while being married. Openly." He said, "I didn't even care. I wanted people to see so I wouldn't have to hide anymore. No masks."

If I'm honest, I've been there. I was there. My there is what drove me to write this book. I've heard myself say in a number of situations, "I'm exhausted. I'm depleted. I've given everything of value, everything of substance, to everyone else. The only thing I ask is for somebody to either say, 'Thank you' or to show appreciation."

It was at that moment, if I wasn't careful, that everything could have taken an awful turn. It got bad...but it could have been much worse.

It's in these moments that too many of us act out.

When you give everything you have, all the time, with no boundaries, the thing you are giving becomes common. And when a person feels common, it's easy to look for the place where you're not common. Weariness desensitizes you and opens the door for you to make decisions that you would normally never make if you were spiritually healthy. Weariness has you in conversation with people that have no good intended for you—because you want to feel uncommon. You want to feel like the winner. No matter that these people aren't pushing you into the callings and destiny of God. The fullness of your flesh takes over, and that can be incredibly dangerous.

The enemy plays with our minds. When we get weary, we start making decisions based on the immediate needs of that moment: the need for affection; the need for validation; the need for celebration. Bottom line? The need to feel seen. When you're weary, those are very real needs. There's nothing wrong with any of them. But if they're met in illegitimate ways, they can hijack what God wants to do in your life.

Ask David and Samson

In the spring, at the time when kings go off to war, David sent Joab out with the king's men and the whole Israelite army. They destroyed the Ammonites and besieged Rabbah. But David remained in Jerusalem.

One evening David got up from his bed and walked around on the roof of the palace. From the roof he saw a woman bathing. The woman was very beautiful, and David sent someone to find out about her. The man said, "She is Bathsheba, the daughter of Eliam and the wife of Uriah the Hittite." Then David sent messengers to get her. She came to him, and he slept with her. (Now she was purifying herself from her monthly uncleanness.) Then she went back home. (2 Samuel 11:1–4)

It's very hard to win when you're weary. Not impossible, but hard. The Bible says it was the spring when kings went to war. It's what you do. David was tired of doing what kings do. Perhaps he was sick of the monotony. Maybe he was bored with the mundane aspects of going out to battle. Or maybe he had gotten so used to winning that he was like, "I'm gonna just chill." He let his guard down, and there was Bathsheba.

Who is that woman taking a bath? What's her name? That's Uriah's wife. Well, tell her to come here.

When you're weary, you make choices that can devastate you. I told you that this is the lie of the enemy. He wants us to make moves based on our appetites, our fleshly inclinations, the things that we see. He wants us moving by sight, and not faith.

> Some time later, he [Samson] fell in love with a woman in the Valley of Sorek whose name was Delilah. The rulers of the Philistines went to her and said, "See if you can lure him into showing you the secret of his great strength and how we can overpower him so we may tie him up and subdue him. Each one of us will give you eleven hundred shekels of silver." So Delilah said to Samson, "Tell me the secret of your great strength and how you can be tied up and subdued." (Judges 16:4–6)

Like David, Samson learned the hard way. He was not a man to be played with. Samson was also a warrior. And his parents were so committed. They loved him so much, they even said, "Son, why don't you choose a wife from your people?" (See Jud. 14.)

Samson was like, "Nah, get me one of them other women. She pleases me." Weak parents and gifted kids… Whew, what a dangerous combination! When you're so enamored with the gift you were called to raise, it's easy to end up worshiping it.

Samson let his guard down, and there was Delilah.

Tell me the secret of your great strength.

This picture of a brawny Samson that we are given in Sunday school is not accurate. His strength wasn't in his muscles. It was in his follicles. The follicles carried the vow—that no razor should touch his hair. In the moment he gave his secret to the wrong one, the glory departed. That's why the Bible says the Lord left him. The glory departed because he gave the sacred thing to the enemy. He bought the stew. He sold his birthright.

> Then she called, "Samson, the Philistines are upon you!" He awoke from his sleep and thought, "I'll go out as before and shake myself free." But he did not know that the LORD had left him. (Judges 16:20)

How much is that stew again? Samson did not know that the Lord had left him. In my estimation, it is the most profound, frightening Scripture in all of the Bible. Nothing scares me more. It scares me because I see a lot of Samson in me. I see a lot of David in me. I see a lot of Esau in me.

That stew is no joke. It tastes good going down. It's a tasty death. It's a tasty end. You dab the corners of your mouth, because it satisfies in that moment. In an instant, though, everything is changed. It's all gone.

es a person of faith to spot his or her own wea-
d say: "Don't make a decision right now. You're
not in a sound place. You're not walking in wisdom. You're
not walking in discretion. You're not walking in authority.
Don't make a decision right now. This is not the time to
make a decision."

What happened with David wasn't about Bathsheba.
What happened with Samson wasn't all about Delilah's
deception. Esau's circumstance was less about Jacob's trick-
ery (we've discussed that some and we'll discuss it more) than
about Esau's exhaustion. Esau was so tired that he treated
what was given to him without effort as common and was
willing to let it go. When you're weary, you lack vision, yes,
but you also lack perspective. You lack understanding. Why
in the world would you give your birthright away for a pot of
stew? You're not that hungry. Essentially what you're saying
is "I don't value what's been given because I didn't have to
work to get it. All I had to do was come out first." Esau was
born first. Maybe he didn't understand the value of what he
had because he didn't earn it.

There's Something about Working for It

Aren't most of us like Esau? My kids don't understand
what they have. I noticed a few months ago that they were
beginning to be more demanding. In my eyes, they weren't
moving as fast when I told them to move. So I started

disciplining them, so they would understand better that what Daddy says goes. I started teaching them that you speak to your elders with respect. That meant "Yes, sir" or "No, ma'am." It meant "Excuse me?" and "Please." I had to have a serious talk with them: "Don't you ever talk to an adult without honor and respect. Don't think that you're entitled because I made a good life for you. This is what I've chosen to do, but you didn't earn this. You haven't done anything to get it." So I have to teach my children the value of humility and thanksgiving for what they've been given, so that they do not treat it commonly. And I think this is often how God deals with us.

The Holy Spirit can heal the wounded, weary soul. He can meet our needs. We've got to be careful of the meals that are presented when we're weary. What we must learn from Esau is that temporary hunger is not worth an eternal promise. We can learn that if we don't take time to rest, refresh, recharge, then the mirage could cause us to ascribe a level of value and intrigue to a thing that it doesn't really have.

If Esau had understood his birthright, he would've weighed its value versus that bowl of stew and kicked that bowl right off the table. He would have said to his sneaky brother, "I'd never sell my birthright. Are you crazy? I'd rather starve. I'll go outside. I'll eat leaves. I'll suck on tree bark before I give you this birthright. Are you crazy?"

But he didn't. The Bible says he despised his birthright. It's not that he didn't want his birthright, but he didn't value it. He didn't value it because he didn't spend enough time with God to understand what it was.

Esau had something in his hands that was eternal and spiritual, but because he was temporal and carnal, he could not see it, nor could he value it properly. Weariness causes us to lack perspective and ascribe a lesser value to things than we should. Or, on the flip side, sometimes when we are weary, we place a value on something that it should never have. Esau realistically traded millions of dollars of wealth and influence as Isaac's firstborn for a bowl of soup. The soup was valued way more than it should have been. Oh, what a dangerous trade!

But that's what spiritual and emotional exhaustion will do. Spiritual and emotional weariness will have you trading things that don't have equal value. Again, allow me some room here, but Esau essentially told Jacob, "I'm going to give you the thing that will define my entire family line for the next six thousand years in exchange for something that I'll crap out of my body later tonight."

And we're not any better than Esau. How many of us have been lonely and found ourselves in the company of individuals who didn't deserve the words of our heart? They hadn't earned our vulnerability, and yet, in our desperation, in our unwillingness to wait on God, there we are, pouring out our souls—right into the pit of the enemy. How many of us have given something of tremendous value to people who could not process it, digest it, or reciprocate?

If a relationship is to have value, there has to be a place of exchange and understanding. But when we're weary and can't see straight, we open our mouths to the wrong people. We form alliances that are not beneficial. We actually begin to take what's valuable and assume that another person can see it and appreciate it. We assume that what they're giving us back is equal in value, and it's not. For whatever reason, the words of Esau rang true, when he said, "What is this birthright to me when I'm about to die?" You're not about to die. You're not that hungry. But you, Esau, are a man ruled by your appetites.

Pay Attention to the Source of Your Hunger

We should be mindful of people who will sell it all for one moment. These are those of us who are ruled by our desires. When you're weary, your carnal appetites win. This is an area I know well. I've always seen a correlation between the food I eat and the sins of my flesh. When I would battle between fasting and praying, I would watch my moods change and things shift. I'd be so angry and hostile during fasting because my body was not used to a boundary. It wasn't used to being told, "No."

I also noticed that as my flesh got weaker, my spirit got stronger. You might think that this should have been obvious to a preacher, but for me it was such a profound revelation. Fasting revealed to me how off I was in the spirit. It showed me where I lacked physical discipline, yes, but the root was not physical. It was spiritual. The places where I struggled were not flesh or physical in nature. They were spiritual in nature.

The need to appease our carnal appetites as a result of weariness has killed way too many of our relationships and dreams. In that state, we trade long-term benefits for short-term pleasure. This especially shows up in premature intimacy. There are people who have given their bodies in a moment, out of a deep carnal hunger, and once that moment was gone, it was exactly that—gone. What you gave was so valuable, and yet the person you gave it to didn't have to work for it. You attached no value to it, so why should they?

I must admit that I've always been fascinated by people who have casual sex. Maybe *fascinated* isn't the word. More like curious. They meet someone and immediately end up having sex. I remember watching some reality show many years ago, in which a woman and some football player went on a date. That night, they slept together.

So this is where I could go all biblical on you and talk about how God doesn't condone premarital sex, etc., etc., blah, blah, blah. All of that would be true, but there was something even more confusing to me about this:

It was the first night. He doesn't know her mother. She hadn't met his family. They didn't have a chance to talk about hopes and dreams, her aspirations or his. They didn't know each other's HIV status. They didn't know anything. And yet they felt that in a two-hour date there was enough information to trade the deepest place of intimate exchange that two human beings can have? Have we devalued sex that much?

I know this is common. I know it happens over and over again. Teenagers sleep with somebody and then potentially regret it for the rest of their lives, because what they did at fifteen has affected them at twenty-five. I've observed so many people in my life and my family who have made that trade, and it's an unfair one, at best.

I remember when I was growing up and my mother would make sandwiches for me to take to school. It was always food I didn't like. Like pepper loaf. Who eats pepper loaf at twelve? If you don't know what it is, consider yourself blessed and highly favored of the Lord. It was a kind of bologna, but it had, like, pieces of green and red peppers in it.

Why though?

Anyway, my mother would put it on some white bread with another anomaly of my childhood: fake mayonnaise—something called Spin Blend dressing. Off to school I went.

People would try to trade food sometimes. If you had good things, you would try to trade for even better things. But I never had anything good to trade. My lunch was always terrible. And so there were a couple of kids that had some developmental challenges. They had great lunches. Since the people who knew better wouldn't trade with me, I would go to the ones that I could finesse, and I'd be like, "You would love these corn chips in this plastic bag." (They

weren't even Fritos. They were the institutional corn chips.
My mom would get a big bag, grab them out with her hand,
and put them in a sandwich bag.) I'd say to these kids, "I'll
trade them for your Doritos."

Anyway, because those kids didn't know what they had,
I'd be like, "Ooh, this is better than that. You should trade
me." And they'd say, "Okay!" not realizing that I was getting the better end of that bargain.

Yes, I know. Hi, Jacob. My name is John.

Who Are You When You Are Tired?

The enemy uses our weariness to attack our identity. If you
are going to produce glory, there will be attacks from the
enemy. The devil can't stand for God to get glory, so if he
sees the potential for glory, he's going to attack it while you
are weak. The enemy will attack you wherever you have a
weakness. He looks to see if you have allowed your exhaustion with life to cause you to lose sight of your end goal.
He's been doing this for thousands of years. Ask Jesus in
the wilderness:

> Then Jesus was led by the Spirit into the wilderness
> to be tempted by the devil. After fasting forty days
> and forty nights, he was hungry. The tempter came
> to him and said, "If you are the Son of God, tell
> these stones to become bread." Jesus answered, "It is

written: 'Man shall not live on bread alone, but on every word that comes from the mouth of God.'"

Then the devil took him to the holy city and had him stand on the highest point of the temple. "If you are the Son of God," he said, "throw yourself down. For it is written: 'He will command his angels concerning you, and they will lift you up in their hands, so that you will not strike your foot against a stone.'" Jesus answered him, "It is also written: 'Do not put the Lord your God to the test.'"

Again, the devil took him to a very high mountain and showed him all the kingdoms of the world and their splendor. "All this I will give you," he said, "if you will bow down and worship me." Jesus said to him, "Away from me, Satan! For it is written: 'Worship the Lord your God, and serve him only.'"

Then the devil left him, and angels came and attended him. (Matthew 4:1–11)

So the Bible says, "After forty days and forty nights, he was hungry." Then the devil comes and says, "If you are the son of God, command these stones to become bread." What's clear to me here is that the devil is trying to figure out if Jesus knows who He is. And if He does know who He is, would He be willing to use His power incorrectly and prematurely for His own selfish motives? Would He be willing, like Esau before him, to trade His divine calling to appeal to His human desires? Jesus responded by declaring, "It is written."

One of the keys to combating weariness is to have a clear vision. Don't just hold that vision in your mind, though, because frankly, not everyone's mental willpower is strong. Your mind is terribly susceptible to succumbing to your physical hungers. Your vision must be established. It has to be written. I encourage you to write down your vision and make it plain, as Habakkuk tells us (see Hab. 2:2). Put in stone your vision. Say to yourself, "These are the pillars that I live and die on. This is who I am." That's how you combat the inevitable weariness that comes with life. That's how you deal with your hunger.

Posterize your dreams. Posterize your goals. Put them in places where you can see them. There will come a time when you'll need to be refreshed and reminded of where you're trying to go. Weariness is coming. But don't let weariness change your trajectory like Esau did.

Evil Esau?

Here's the thing: Esau was not an evil person. There's nothing in Scripture that says that Esau was mean to Jacob prior to the stealing of the birthright. If anything, Scripture shows he was oblivious. The mistake he made was that Jacob wasn't even on his radar. He was the little brother. But the idea that Esau was this evil being that was messing with Jacob is false. Sure, it would make the story a little more exciting when Jacob gets the blessing, but the Bible doesn't say that. What we see with Esau is a man who was so privileged, so used to getting what he wanted, that the stuff that should have mattered to him didn't.

It's important for us to realize that God is not impressed with our status. He's not moved by what tradition or society has determined should be ours. He's not checking for degrees or diplomas, nor is He evaluating the kind of jobs we have or how many zeros are on our paychecks. People may revere us. They may say we deserve first place. They may pump our heads up with all kinds of unsubstantiated praise about who we are or should be. But the only thing that really matters is what God wants from our lives. When we become comfortable with the status given to us by the world, we leave ourselves susceptible to making a life-changing mistake, like Esau.

Your History Matters

Because of the oral traditions prominent in Hebrew culture, Jacob and Esau knew about the history of their people: where they came from; the story of Abraham and their father, Isaac. Jewish history is filled with instances where stories were told and passed down for generations. Much of the Bible is the later transcription of stories and recollections of events passed down through the oral tradition.

So Esau forgoing his birthright was actually a slap in the face of that history. Honoring the journey of our ancestors gives context and value to our future. In those times when we are weary, we realize that this plan God has working didn't start with us and, if we live right, it won't end with us.

When I think about the life I've been privileged to live, I think about the fact that my mother bought her first home when I was twenty. I took my first flight when I was seventeen. I was in my twenties when I took my first international flight. I think about my four-year-old son and three-year-old daughter who have traveled to Australia and New Zealand this year. They have passports, and they've been stamped. They have their own luggage. They have status on the airlines. My son is almost gold. My daughter is silver. Premier silver at four, and they have traveled around this nation and around the world.

None of this was something I could have imagined for myself growing up. I come from a very different place. My grandmother would catch the bus to work. I remember at the first of the month, three of my uncles and my grandmother were always waiting for the mailman to give them checks from the government. These were mustard-colored envelopes, and you could see the check with the Statue of Liberty on it on the inside. They were so happy that they were getting these checks from the government.

I remember blocks of cheese being delivered. I remember

my one-legged grandfather, who used to be a preacher, sending me a toy monkey that played the drums and cymbals at the same time—it came in the mail with a handwritten letter. I remember listening to him on the phone and realizing maybe for the first time that I come from a history of people who were poor.

My grandmother didn't have enough money for a house, but she walked into a house, slammed her hand on the mantel of the fireplace, and said, "God, I thank you for my house." She didn't have much money but she had a giant faith. I can still hear the inflection in her voice when she told me and my cousins the story. My mother and her brother, my Uncle Eddie, signed and cosigned for my grandmother to get the house at 39 Twenty-Ninth Street in Cincinnati. She got it because she believed that she could get it, and it's that history that really informs me. It's those stories that remind me that the privileges I'm able to give my children are not anything I've done myself. I didn't get here by myself.

The Bible says that we are surrounded by a great cloud of witnesses (see Heb. 12:1). For my sports fans, Hebrews 12 is essentially saying there's a stadium in heaven, and our grandmothers who prayed for us, our granddaddies who prayed for us, our mama who went on to be with Jesus, our great-uncles and aunties and other loved ones who were saved by the blood of Jesus, are all now in the stands looking down and cheering us on.

In African traditions, we always honor our ancestors. I know that what I'm doing and how I'm living was not conceivable to them. It's that legacy that keeps me alive. So many times, I've wanted to give up. I've wanted to quit. How many nights did I ask God not to wake me up because I felt wholly disqualified for how God was using me? And I know I'm not alone. There are millions of people who feel the same way. But the one thing I have to remember is that I didn't make me. God did. He chose me to be birthed with the lineage and heritage I had. And when God says we are enough, we must believe Him.

There is another way our history shows up for us. I remember driving home after a heavy petting session with a woman I had a crush on. I'd turned down sex with the woman and had to endure the embarrassment that comes for every nineteen-year-old male virgin when you tell a woman that the reason why you won't have sex with her is because she isn't your wife. Anyway, I didn't live that far, so the drive was short, but I still arrived home around midnight. I walked into the apartment where I lived with my mother and decided not to go and greet her because I felt such heavy shame.

Then, years later, my mother said something that blew my mind. She said, "Every night when you would leave, I would pray." She said, "The Lord would tell me to pray for you. I would pray that you wouldn't make a decision that would cost you your future. It actually got to the point where I said to God, 'I'm tired of praying for my son.' But

God gave me the strength to keep praying for you because I knew what you were supposed to do and who you're supposed to be."

So my understanding of the impact of history and heritage comes from knowing that I am the product of a woman who would not stop praying, even when I was actively trying to find ways to sin. She prayed that my life would not be altered, and that I wouldn't make a decision because I was "tired of waiting" that would change everything. That is the danger of weariness.

Esau made a permanent decision based on temporary hunger, but I'm not beating him up, because I've been there. The authentic narrative of my life is that I am the embodiment of duality. There is a part of me that desires God. Then there's a part of me that doesn't want to be bothered with God at all. There's a part of me that wants to see the people of God coming to the knowledge of Jesus. And then there are times when I don't even want to go home because the pressure is too great. But it's my history that holds me.

The legacy of my entire family is on the line when I make a decision, just as it was for Esau. In my family, men don't stay. They leave. They've all left. I've seen the legacy that was left behind by men who were supposed to stay and couldn't. By men who were supposed to be present. I don't want to repeat their mistakes. I also came from a legacy of women who made God decisions, so that's where I stake my claim. I'm a man who is striving to make God decisions.

The Grace of God Covers Us

I don't know why Isaac couldn't reverse what happened with Jacob and Esau in both instances: the soup and the scheme with Rebekah, the blessing and the birthright. I've always wondered about that. They weren't yet living under Mosaic law, so I've always been curious about why Jacob's fraudulent actions weren't corrected. It's entirely possible, though, that Isaac saw these deceptions as somehow aligning with the prophecy spoken over the twins at birth.

Whatever the reason, what I do know is that God's forgiveness and grace doesn't always come without consequence. Maybe this was Esau's. Scripture does tell us that Esau cried out for his father's blessing, and that might be our starting point for thinking about how to deal with the aftermath of our "bad trades."

> Esau said to his father, "Have you but one blessing, my father? Bless me, even me also, O my father." And Esau lifted up his voice and wept. (Genesis 27:38 ESV)

God graces us when we trade our long-term benefits for short-term pleasure. I'm a living witness. That doesn't mean we don't pay the consequences for our actions. It does mean that God still loves us and still wants to set us on the path He has determined from the beginning. As believers, we often are taught to beat ourselves up when our urges, this flesh, reveal themselves. Men and women are hiding out in churches, condemned by their secret sins, simply because they feel unable to talk about them and live in the fullness of their redemption. Repentance is absolutely necessary. But afterward too many of us are living in condemnation. We cry out, "How can God love me?" We believe that we are eternally lost. I know I've believed that more times than I can count.

> There is therefore now no condemnation for those who are in Christ Jesus. (Romans 8:1 ESV)

Thank God for our Lord and Savior, Jesus. He never let my urges be my end, and He won't let yours be either.

I remember talking to one of my good brothers in Christ. He's been married now for over twenty years. He'd shared with me his battle with a porn addiction while he was married. He felt like he had to hide it, and so he nursed that shame for many years. By the grace of God, he eventually confessed it to his wife. They got counseling and began to heal. Today, their marriage is thriving and is evidence of the availability of God's grace when we trade long-term benefit for short-term pleasure. It's the grace of God that says, "I love you, and I won't allow your bad decision here to define your forever."

In the case of Esau, there was no Mosaic law in place. But there were laws and traditions that were upheld. Isaac basically said, "It's an unbreakable oath. It's a covenant. It's done." In other words, "This is a legally binding declaration. I can't give you what you've given away."

But we're not under those laws. We're under grace. That grace has kept me and you. All of us, in our weariness, have made bad decisions. And in that moment, you lost. You lost integrity. It might even feel like you lost a little bit of your soul. But God says, "I'm going to use this loss to help you win, if you let Me. I'm not going to let this loss define you."

CHAPTER FOUR

Blind Ambition

We all think we need ambition to win. But more often than not, selfish ambition keeps us losing in the areas of our lives that matter most.

Ambition in our culture tells us, "Go get it!" You have to be stronger, faster, and work harder than anyone else. You've got to do what another person won't do. You need to be "gangster" and "cutthroat." And while you're at it, be passionate but show no real emotion. Empathy is a weakness—it must be all about you and your needs And in the context of our culture, you've gotta go get it, you've gotta be stronger, you've gotta be faster, you've gotta work harder, you've gotta do what the other person won't do, and you've gotta be cutthroat, and you've gotta be gangster with it, and you've gotta be all of these different things, and you've gotta be emotionless, but you've gotta be passionate at the same time, but you can't be weak, and you can't show empathy, and it's about you.

That is so far from what God intended.

So much of what we call ambition is really a response to the things that are absent in our lives. For Jacob, I suspect it was the hope of being accepted. For me it was the absence of my father. I talk quite a bit about this because so much of who I am—the deficits that I'm constantly working through—has been informed by my father's absence. It's driven an ambition that sometimes does not align with my purpose and intended identity.

Prepared for Purpose, Prepared on Purpose

For many of us, the foundational questions of our existence are: What is my purpose? What am I here for? Why did God create me? Why do I have certain gifts? It's critical that we take an accurate self-assessment in order to begin this journey toward being our authentic selves. In this assessment, we will uncover the things that make up the unique individual that we are and check the selfish ambition that has the potential to rise up in us. We do this so that we are able to embrace the totality of who God created us to be. Once we are able to embrace who God called us to be, there is no room to be insecure or jealous of someone else. There is no need to be so driven by ambition that we are willing to, like Jacob, steal for it. We are not in competition with anyone else. There is nothing about what someone else is doing that will be an indicator of your success. Like Jacob, you have a word over your life. That word will not change and doesn't require your manipulations to make it come to pass. In fact, the success metric for a believer is actually this: Am I being obedient to the voice of the Holy Ghost? Am I doing what the Lord wants me to do? There are talents we may have that are no indication of who God has called us to be. He is intentional with us.

Yes, you were prepared for purpose—the purposes of God. The big picture. But you were also prepared *on* purpose. This means everything that has happened in your life had an assignment. God wants to shift us in many of the same ways he did Jacob, so that what's inside of us can manifest. Does that mean you're going to get the corner office? Maybe. But it might mean you will have more responsibilities and more influence over more people. And as you get more influence, God may allow you favor with people who will see how hard you work, sense the anointing on your life, and facilitate the opening of doors. Be open to what those open doors look like.

I can't recall the number of times people have said, "Hey, man, you're funny. You should do comedy! You should go to Hollywood and do the Laugh Factory." But that ability to make people laugh is bigger than the singular talent of telling jokes on a stage. Yes, maybe I can make those three hundred people at the comedy club laugh, but I can also bring the joy of the Lord into the sanctuary on a Wednesday night or Sunday morning. So many things that look like God opportunities—like open doors—are not. We must be discerning in this season of our lives. Counterfeit options and opportunities are always waiting to take us off track.

So we shouldn't get sad and concerned that no one sees our hard work right now. God is going to allow the right people at the right moment to see what you're doing, and in the right time, He's going to shift you into overdrive. We must stay faithful though. That's what it means to be prepared on purpose.

The Things I Missed

There was so much I needed to know. What did it mean to become a man? What does that look like? How do I talk to women? How do I engage in intellectual conversations? What does it mean to be street smart? For me, the absence of my father shaped me as much as his presence. I saw him four times and I remember each one. But I also remember the times when I wanted to have access to him and he wasn't there. My first kiss, right outside of Gold Circle Cinema on Ridge Road in Cincinnati. I started kissing this girl after the movie and my mother pulled up, so yes, technically the kiss was one, maybe two seconds. Whatever. The raging hormones of an emerging teenager were in full effect. There were so many emotions, and the only safe place to put them was in the hands and heart of my mother.

So the filter for my manhood came from a woman. A Christian woman. A morally upright Christian woman raising a boy in a society that was very different from the one in which she grew up. It was the beginning of hip-hop. There was an emergence of a drug culture. And as much as I loved my mother, revered her, I wanted my dad. I just wanted him near me. My ambition was to be like him.

My ambition, like so much of what we call ambition nowadays, was defined by the hole in my heart.

My mother talked to me about this, many years later. She said, "I knew that you wanted to be around your father so bad. You so wanted your father in your life that no matter what he did, good or bad, you would have done it also." She then told me something that many mothers would have taken to their graves. "I knew how much you idolized him and, well, I asked God to keep him from you. And God answered my prayer. Because I'm one hundred percent sure that you would not have turned out to be the same man you are, if He hadn't."

My mother knew that I was so desperate for validation from my father that I would have done whatever it took to please him. My ambition was blinded by my need. Ambition just wants what it wants. I wanted to be accepted by my father, so I would have done whatever it took to be accepted.

This kind of ambition does what it takes to get what it

wants. It really is blind, because you are not looking at any-thing except for what you want. You don't care about the consequences. Not just for yourself, but for anybody else. It is rooted in a level of individual carnality. It's unchecked ambition and unsubmitted, and it shows up in our world in numerous ways. It's why people cheat to win races and on tests. Their blind ambition drives them to want to look smart and be first. They want to be perceived as the best, whether they actually are or not.

Jacob, Jesus, and Me

> This is my beloved Son, in whom I am well pleased.
> (Matthew 3:17 KJV)

Whenever I hear the story of Jesus' baptism and God's proclamation over Him, I always have one question: If Jesus is the well-pleasing son, then who am I? Because I certainly don't look like Him. And though I know I'm supposed to, I don't function like Him.

If there was one person who could wield His power in a way that would give Him exactly what He wanted, it was Jesus. And yet He had the most power with the least per-sonal ambition. Instead of blind ambition, Jesus was blind *to* ambition. He had no desire to build anything to himself. Jesus' sole desire was to serve at the request of His Father; to do the will of His Father. He wasn't working *for* validation,

He was working *from* validation. That's the biggest difference between the ambition our culture tells us to have and how God wants us to move through our journeys. Jesus never wondered if He was accepted. And the only time we see a place of tumult or unrest was in the garden of Gethsemane when He asks for the cup to pass (see Matt. 26:42), and on the cross when He cries out in Matt. 27:46, "Eloi, Eloi, lama sabachthani?" (My God, my God, why have you forsaken me?)

Those are the words of a man who is saying to his father, "Are you still with me? I've done what you've asked me to do, but I don't feel your presence. I don't feel your favor." Jesus felt that disconnect, of being cut off from the Father, so we would never have to.

(Feel free to shout right here. I'll wait.)

So, two times. That's it. Jesus didn't need ambition, because He was secure in who He was and what He'd been called to do. I'll readily admit that this kind of security is hard to grasp. Especially when one considers the cost.

I have achieved what some consider success in this world of ministry. I've traveled the globe and preached at many of the largest churches in the world. I have standing invitations to some of the most influential conferences and moves of God. I have a bunch of stuff and lots of opportunity but have had to ask myself on a regular basis, "Why am I so sad?"

I now know why. Sadness is what happens when you run, run, run, chasing what you think will make you happy. It's where I've found myself and I suspect where Jacob found himself. Perhaps he started like me. Maybe Jacob said, "I just want my dad to see me. I want that birthright, then maybe I'll have a relationship with my father, like Esau." And then when that didn't work, when the methods he employed to get what he wanted backfired, not only did he lose his relationship with his brother, he also lost his relationships with his father and his mother. Yes, even Rebekah. The one who saw him. The one who plotted with him to get the birthright blessing from Isaac. She ends up telling him, "You have to leave or your brother's going to kill you."

Jacob lost his family over ambition. He wanted something that didn't belong to him, and he was willing to lose it all to get it.

In My Performance, I Trust

I've been faced with the tremendous costs of some of the decisions I've made. This is especially true at the most challenging point in my marriage, when Aventer was going to seek a divorce because of my lack of vision, commitment, and protection of her heart and my family. Blind ambition will cause you to treat people poorly. You might be kind to strangers out of some understanding of decorum, but you'll be incredibly mean to your family. Jacob's ambition was so blind that Leah, his own wife, every time she had a child, would say, "Now he'll love me. Maybe now he'll love me."

Only after birthing her fourth son, Judah, did she say, "Now I'm going to praise the Lord." The whole time she's bearing children and thinking that doing so will knit his heart to hers. Jacob, though, was "just not into her." She was just a place for him to sow his seed, not a place of emotional support. She was a physical place of release, nothing more, and she knew it. And the Bible says, "When the Lord saw that she was unloved, He gave her a son" (see Gen. 29:32). And ambition unchecked in the life of any individual will cause those around you to feel unloved.

If you were watching us from the outside, things looked great. We had a show on the Oprah Winfrey Network, positions at the largest church in America, and we'd just been announced as pastors of a brand-new church. People put my face on flyers, and people register for conferences because they know I'm coming.

I learned very quickly that I wasn't just a man, I was an economy. I wasn't just a voice, I was a voice that paid people's bills. And when I became a commodity, God became less of a priority. That's what blind ambition did. It shifted my priorities. I had to ask questions that I now ask you, Reader. Is the presence of God a priority? Is the will of God a priority? Is the work of the kingdom a priority? Or is your idea of winning about the accumulation of things?

In our society, and even in church culture, there's a hierarchy. There are certain preachers and pastors whose names, when people see them on promo materials or on the cover of books, generate a level of excitement. People respond to how we make them feel, maybe even more than what we say. There's a certain entertainment value, and yes, I've been complicit in the perpetuating of that "conference culture."

That's hard to admit.

And it's a hard ride to stop. It's almost like people have been sold tickets to a show, and if I don't perform, then I'm not really part of the circle. Of course, ambition drives my need to be part of the cycle, and so it's a dangerous cycle of self-fulfilling prophecy where if I don't feel fulfilled in this (preaching), I'm not happy, but this is all I know to do, it's what they—forget God—expect of me, so let me do that, despite being unfulfilled and unhealthy in my soul. This machine wasn't really designed for me to be healthy anyway. It's designed for me to perform. Ambition is rooted in performance.

The Ambition Paradox

When he had finished washing their feet, he put on his clothes and returned to his place. "Do you understand what I have done for you?" he asked them. "You call me 'Teacher' and 'Lord,' and rightly so, for that is what I am. Now that I, your Lord and Teacher, have washed your feet, you also should wash one another's feet. I have set you an example that you should do as I have done for you. Very truly I tell you, no servant is greater than his master, nor is a messenger greater than the one who sent him. Now that you know these things, you will be blessed if you do them." (John 13:12–17)

The objective of ambition is to perform at the highest level. The objective of the kingdom is to serve at the lowest level. This means that no matter the size of your gift, you serve those who are at the lowest level. Now we have this great juxtaposition between what God wants you to do with your ambition and what the world wants you to do. Jacob wanted it all. He wanted a double portion, the birthright, he wanted it all! And when he couldn't get it being himself, he manipulated, cajoled, and connived to obtain it. That cost him a great deal.

Ambition will always cost you if you don't submit it. No matter what's in front of you, no matter who you are, God will allow ambition to be an option for you—only so you can release it to Him. That's the paradox. We must submit our ambitions to God. We must be willing to say, "No, I'm not gonna get it *that* way."

If Jesus had been so ambitious that He was willing to skirt the process, He could have done that back in Matthew, when he was tempted by the devil in the wilderness. He could have worshiped the devil at the top of that mountain. If He had, He would have learned the truth that all of us learn when we try to obtain success through selfish ambition. It doesn't work. Jesus wouldn't have gotten anything that the devil promised Him, because the devil is a liar. He makes us believe he will do what he says, but the only one with that kind of consistency is God. Remember that when the devil whispers in your ear that you must do something evil in order to live. He'll lie and say that you're going to die. He's a liar. He wants to kill you. He's like a roaring lion seeking whomever he may devour. He comes to steal, kill, and destroy, but if you are in Christ, you have life, and life more abundantly (see John 10:10).

Ambition seeks to be celebrated. Unchecked ambition seeks to be puffed up. But Christ-centered ambition is very different—if we can call it ambition at all. We should seek to be as ambitious as Jesus, who said, "My will is to do the will of my Father. I have meat that you know not of. I'm in another place. I'm only about the kingdom" (see John 4:32–34). His will—and subsequently His ambition—was submitted to the Father.

Here is the most powerful man to ever walk the earth. He invested all of His divinity to redeem our humanity. Jesus is healing the sick, raising the dead, casting out demons, and stretching out withered hands. He's stopping the issue of blood in a woman who's been sick for twelve years, while simultaneously healing a little girl who was twelve years old and dead. His fame was spreading. Nowadays he would have "gone viral." He was popular. He could easily have created a kingdom of the traditional variety, a coalition of strong men. Instead, He chose to pour himself into twelve regular men, one of whom He knew would betray Him. For some, that was a loser move. But Jesus was going after the greater win. He did that so that one day these regular men could build something that would outlast His season wrapped in flesh.

What a strange, beautiful picture of God-led ambition. We should live exactly this way. Our constant prayer should be, "Lord, I want to live my life in such a way that, when I die, what I leave behind is enough for your kingdom to expand." Think about the ministries we see all around us. Too many ministry leaders are faced with the prospect that if they died, their ministries would die with them. Their ambition prevents them from putting together a succession plan. They refuse to raise up anyone who could build, expound upon, and extend the ministry in any way.

Ambition Doesn't Satisfy

When I examine my life, I realize that I've been given a lot. One of my spiritual fathers, Bishop Donald Clay, once said to me, "God has given you everything early so you could see that none of it can satisfy you." I'm learning how true that is. No platform, no material thing, matters if I'm looking past my wife or if I think of my children as an inconvenience to me watching ESPN. I, like so many of us, must come face-to-face with my unhealthy, unsubmitted ambitions—some of which can be sourced in my childhood.

I wasn't always a preacher. I was a kid growing up in a single-parent home, whose mother had to do the best she could with what she had. We all have things that we dream about. Nice cars used to make my heart skip a beat, because I like cars. That's not carnal. It's just human. I think there are certain things that drive passion that are completely human. They're not necessarily a spiritual indicator of how we value people, our calling, God. None of that. I just like cars. I've always liked cars. When I had nothing, I liked cars. But as I matured and grew older, I was able to acquire the cars that were the cars of my dreams. Then there are houses. I remember driving past a house one day and say- ing, "Man, that would be nice to own a home one day," and now the Lord has blessed me to have a home for my wife and my kids that is amazing.

But even after I got that house and filled it with furni- ture, I still wasn't happy. I was perpetually unhappy. I'm the associate pastor of the largest single-building church in the United States, preaching to thousands, and I would go home profoundly unhappy. My questions were always the same: Did I make my mark? Does this even matter? Were people even listening? Have I changed? The truth is, none of the things I've mentioned satisfies the longing of the soul.

We can run like Jesse Owens after things, and God will continue to say, "None of it will satisfy you. In fact, I love you so much I'm gonna let you have it all just so you can see how empty it makes you feel." Consider this: If money sat- isfied us, would rich people ever commit suicide? If material trappings could give us peace, would prescription drugs be abused by the wealthy and the famous? And trust me, I recognize the privilege I have in even posing these questions from this perspective. But the truth, whether you are rich and famous or still climbing the corporate ladder, is that there's a longing in the soul that only God can fill.

Ambition is a sacrifice that must be brought to the altar if we are to truly manifest the heart of Jesus. Jesus came to redeem the lost sheep of the house of Israel. Remember… Israel was the name Jacob got after he wrestled with God. But you know what's super exciting about that? When we hear God introduced, it's usually as the God of Abraham, Isaac, and…Jacob. Not Abraham, Isaac, and Israel. That's the redemption at work! It's like God is saying, "That one that was a mess? I'm the God of that guy. I'm the God of the guy with ambition. I'm the God of the guy that will cheat you." And so I'm glad that He's the God of the part of us that doesn't always get it right; that doesn't always see things properly; that's more concerned with the celebration of strangers than the honor that comes with being a worthy and honorable spouse and parent, a person of integrity and character.

Getting to Who We Really Are

When we submit our ambition to God, what we get is an accurate picture of who we really are. And it is from that place of humility that we serve people. Jesus served because He knew who He was in His Father, and He knew His calling. He was not moved by the shouts of people. He never "committed Himself to men." Man will celebrate you one day and crucify you the next. Jesus taught us that we cannot function for the celebration of people. We can't function with this win-at-all-costs attitude given to us by our culture. This is the challenge of my life now, and it will likely be my challenge for the rest of my life. Yet, if there is a singular ambition we should all have, it's this: to do the will of the Father so that, at some point, we hear Him say, "Well done."

CHAPTER FIVE

Running for Your Life

Once Jacob got the birthright and Esau found out what had happened, Esau determined, "I'm going to kill him." So, at their mother's prompting, Jacob ran.

How many of us would rather run from the messes we've made than face ourselves and the people we've hurt? Our unsubmitted ambitions will often lead us to compromise our integrity. Inevitably, though, those tricks blow up in our faces. We thought we won, but our win was actually a disqualification. You got the prize—maybe even the thing that God ordained for you—but you didn't get it the right way. And the consequence for that is you are now on the run.

Too many of us don't deal well with accountability. We prefer the low-hanging fruit in our lives, the things that are easy to address or deal with. Or, like Jacob, we believe ourselves to be wise and tricky, and so we deflect and redirect, pointing people in the direction of something or someone else while we make our escape. As I've shared in this book, I know more than I care to admit about that.

If we are going to be winners that God can use, that God can and will honor, then our victories must be rooted in truth. Jacob was not a man who embraced truth. Instead of embracing the truth, he ran. And when we run, we learn pretty quickly that we have acquired a birthright that we can't access, because the one it actually belongs to is coming to kill us. When the thing we didn't address properly is chasing us, it's time to change our strategy.

Life Comes at You Fast

> Esau held a grudge against Jacob because of the blessing his father had given him. He said to himself, "The days of mourning for my father are near; then I will kill my brother Jacob." When Rebekah was told what her older son Esau had said, she sent for her younger son Jacob and said to him, "Your brother Esau is planning to avenge himself by killing you. Now then, my son, do what I say: Flee at once to my brother Laban in Harran." (Genesis 27:41–43)

When we run toward something in blind ambition, we might run with it for a while, but ultimately we end up running *from* it.

In my past, I've often run from the responsibilities that come with my development as a man. It's funny to write this now, but my wife always says to me, "Why don't you open the mail?" That seems like such a simple thing—except that it isn't. It goes much deeper and stems from a season in my life when I refused to face the reality of the bills I created. Something as simple as not opening mail turned into not paying bills on time, which then affected my credit, my ability to purchase things I really needed, and my good name. I actually thought, *If I don't open them, they will handle themselves.* That's not faith, by the way. That's stupidity. Bills don't go away because you don't open them.

It's funny because, when you get a credit card, you have to sign a statement saying you'll pay on time. You give your word that you will pay. And so your credit is basically a number that is in line with your ability to keep your word. The contract you signed doesn't say "Pay when you can." It says, "Pay every thirty days, on time, and we will report your payment history to a credit agency."

Isn't it interesting, the link between our names and the power of our word? Depending on what it is we've done and how it is we've carried ourselves, certain names carry more weight in some areas than others. When our name is attached to the inability to keep our word, it affects our credibility. To some extent, gifts don't matter at that point. I remember my wife and I having a disagreement and her saying, "You know...the people hear you preach, they hear your gift, but I see you as you are." If I'm honest, I admit that it angered me to hear that. Because essentially what she was saying was that my name might be good in one area—preaching—but my credibility was shot at home.

It's far too easy for us to run toward the thing that comes naturally to us, the stuff that comes easy. The problem is, there are some things that come naturally that also require godly guidance, a supernatural touch.

I might be naturally attracted to multiple women, as I have been for most of my life, but it took God's guidance and supernatural strength to stop me from engaging in what came naturally to me. There is a supernatural enabling power given to us through the Holy Spirit that helps us to navigate our natural inclination to run toward the things that are familiar and safe. It is the spirit of God and the spirit of faith that says, "There's more to life than this."

Introducing: The Big Three

Jacob was literally running for his life. But he was also running *from* his life. He was running from the life he'd orchestrated. This life was not rooted in authenticity or transparency. It wasn't founded on integrity. He had been living on the slippery slope of deceit, and without authenticity, transparency, and integrity—the big three—it was impossible to live a life that honored God.

The psalmist says that God "desires truth in the inward parts" (see Ps. 51:6). Truth is transparency. Does everybody need to know everything about you? No. But if you're ever going to be used by God in any way that is significant, there will be areas of your life that will require transparency. It is not comfortable, nor is it designed to be. But God requires this of us because the types of leaders who have the greatest impact are those who have the capacity to be vulnerable. Today's generation craves people who are unashamed of their flaws, people who embrace their failures and share the stories and lessons learned from them. These are the kind of leaders who understand that even when it feels like there are forces working against us, they're actually not. God is using the pressure. These failures and oppositions are designed to push us. Sometimes we need opposition to go forward. In fact, it's opposition that helps us to understand the power of victory in our forward progress. When we win from within, there is an internal awareness of being victorious in the areas that matter to God. We aren't afraid to share our struggles, because we know that only the opinion of the Father matters in the end.

I know. Our culture celebrates winners, not failures. But that's the problem with the standard of winning set by culture and not by God. It is the failures that make us. We aren't able to even understand the value of a win until we've had many losses. When Jacob was running for his life, from both the physical and emotional perspectives, he was always a wreck. Every single time he had an opportunity to face himself, to face his bad behavior, he would run. Dealing with his issues was likely too hard so, just like us, he found a way around it.

Dealing for Healing

Like Jacob, I've run my whole life. I've run from the necessary discipline of taking care of my physical body. I've mastered the art of masking, redirecting, and deflecting. My technique of choice? Comedy. I can use comedy and comedic elements to make you look over there instead of *here*. I know how to minimize the pain I'm in by laughing about it or making you laugh at something that is actually a great struggle. Comedy, for me, has always been a way to disconnect without appearing to do so. So many people view funny people as open and super transparent. In most cases, it's the exact opposite. Comedy can be used to create distance. Telling jokes or making fun of something means that I don't have to deal with whatever emotions are building inside of me. I can make someone else laugh even as I'm crying on the inside.

My wife, the mirror sent to me by God, will sometimes say, "Everything's not funny." In those moments, I'm sobered. Usually my response is very deadpan: "I know it's not funny. I also know exactly what I'm doing. I don't want to deal with it." I'm completely conscious of when I'm running away from something I need to heal from.

This brings me to an important point: the things you don't deal with, you cannot heal from. If you do not deal, you cannot heal.

If there's a need for healing, then we must acknowledge there's a wounding. Most of us run because we are wounded. Wounded by rejection. Wounded by misinterpretation of our motives. I've been wounded by the need to be loved. There were too many times when I felt completely ignored by the people that mattered the most to me.

When those things happened, instead of addressing them, I ran. Clearly, it's not a physical run. (Don't you dare laugh! Okay, you can laugh a little. See? Comedic deflection in full effect.) Seriously, though, my running was more emotional. It's where I allowed my heart to take off in another direction.

If we keep running long enough, the scenery changes. We can use our talents and gifts to deflect and resist the uncomfortable things we must face about ourselves. People are way too wowed by talent, not realizing that talent alone does not make a man or a woman. It never has and never will. The deflection of pain is all a deception. Our core issues are still there, because the hard truth is this: wherever we run, there we are.

Returning to the Pain

I know what I'm about to say will be hard, but it's necessary: Stop running. But don't just stop. Return to the place you are running from—the wounding place. It's likely in such places you will find your greatest self. Those places are where you'll find your greatest victories. Yes, it's in those painful places where you'll find the fulfillment of your dreams, the vision for your life that seems so elusive.

God is committed to developing us. He desires for us to reflect His glory. Facing our pain, the things we run from, is part of His sanctification process. If we run from the process, we could potentially shift the timetable of our destiny. He's waiting for us to return. He's waiting to help us rewrite our story.

A New Narrative

Have you ever done anything you wish you hadn't done? When we were growing up, we'd play all kinds of games. If the game wasn't working out the way we wanted, we would yell out, "Stop! I want to do over!" Do you ever wish you could have a life do-over? I'm sure there were moments where Jacob wished he'd made a different decision. Maybe then, all that running wouldn't have been necessary. I know, for me, there have been many times when I wished I could change some part of my life, that I could unmake a moment.

Those of us who have been here, we know what it is like to wish we could turn back the hands of time and change our story. We say, "This can't be how it ends." There are things I've done for which I have certainly asked the Lord for forgiveness, and I also have a deep desire to go back and tell the people I hurt how sorry I am, but for whatever reason, that was impossible. We've all heard the stories of someone arguing with a family member and then something tragic happens and that person is never able to say good-bye or "I'm sorry."

We've all been there, right?

Well, here's the hard reality that Jacob had to face, as do we: Life keeps moving. It goes on. It's strange because even though life can often feel coincidental or accidental, there is an intrinsic intentional purpose to every single thing that has happened in our lives—the good, the bad, the ugly. The interconnected supernatural touch of God has brought us into a collective moment even as you and others read this book. God has never been caught off guard by anything that happens on the earth. Everything about our lives has been written. And yet, while God has a plan for our lives, there have still been moments when we could have done something differently. Because we are autonomous human beings with a personal will, we can choose to obey God or not. When we don't, there are consequences. When we choose to live by our own convictions and not the conviction of the Holy Spirit, we will inevitably cry out for a do-over. We can't continue to live by our own personal convictions exclusively, our own conventional wisdom. Our wisdom can take us only so far. We need the Holy Spirit to lead us and guide us so that we can do His will.

Particularly as believers, we do not exist as individuals unto ourselves. We were birthed in the mind of an intentional God that has a purpose for our lives. Remember Hebrews 12? Well, it says in verses 1 and 2, "Let us run with patience the race that is set before us, looking to Jesus the author and finisher of *our* faith" (KJV).

Part of "winning" is recognizing that Jesus is exactly that: the AUTHOR and finisher of our faith. There is so much power in understanding this, so let me explain. When an author writes a story, he or she is in control of the story. If there is something in the story they don't like, they get to revise it. They can change it, amend it, or turn it around. Authors can create new characters in a story because, well, they are the author. The characters were birthed in their imagination. The source of a character's identity comes directly from the author's heart. In the case of our lives, the ones we surrender when we accept Christ as our Lord and Savior, Jesus is the author. We have been written and published by the almighty God.

Sure, there still may be people out there who don't know your story. Maybe they don't get it. They may not be able to feel your pain. But none of that matters, because God isn't finished yet. As long as there is breath in your body, He's still authoring your story. It doesn't matter who tries to write you off. Jacob could have decided not to return home after his season of "life lessons with Laban." He could have accepted the story that the world had tried to write for him. The story of the trickster. The narrative of the manipulator. But God had already written his story. From the prophecy to Rebekah to the dreaming of ladders, there were chapters God was still writing, and he knew it.

CHAPTER SIX

Hi, My Name Is...

Jacob ran because that's what *Jacob* would do. His name spoke for itself. His name meant trickster, con artist. And even if he wanted to escape it, his name defined him. His past actions defined him. And so it goes with us. We are often defined by the worst areas of our life. We are defined by things about ourselves that we wish we could change or things we wish we had done differently. The shame of our past, the guilt of the things that we did wrong, the specter of possibility that those things could come back, hinders us from really walking in victory or living a life that is full and fulfilling. In the case of Jacob, imagine having to introduce yourself by the worst thing you ever did.

"Hi, I am a con man."

"Hi, my name is Heel Grabber."

"Hi, I am Trickster."

This was Jacob's lot, and no matter what he wanted to

be, his name kept pulling him back. It was constraining. No matter how much he wanted to become something else, no matter how much he tried to dream of something else, his name was his identity.

Redefining Our Names

So the man gave names to all the livestock, the birds in the sky and all the wild animals. (Genesis 2:20)

We are all known by our names. Author Ralph Ellison once said, "It is through our names that we first place ourselves in the world. Our names, being the gift of others, must be made our own." But what happens when the meaning of your name and your character are one and the same? We can look throughout Scripture and observe people manifesting the meaning of their name. There is such authority in naming, an authority that comes all the way from Genesis, where we see Adam given his first authority, not over Eve but over naming every plant and animal on the earth. Whatever he named it, that was the name. And more importantly, it functioned based on what he called it.

In all his running, Jacob could not escape his name. He manifested his name because I imagine introducing yourself as a con man and trickster does something to your psyche. Your sense of identity. The expression of who you are. People are already giving you the side-eye as soon as you say, "Hi, my name is…" Before you ever do a thing, you're already defined by what you've been called. Like Adam's plants and animals, you begin to function based on what you are called.

So how do we allow this realization of what we manifest by our names to be redefined by God? First, we must understand that the original declaration of our names doesn't have to be our final identity. The power of God can change the narrative associated with who we've been, and even extract value out of any negative connotations. God knew what Jacob would do, and it still didn't cause God to choose someone else.

God knew he was a trickster. He knew everything about him. Then, in essence, God said, "I can work with him, because at least he's honest about his lies." When Jacob stopped running, he chose not to hide who he was anymore.

Put Away the Measuring Stick

It's actually refreshing when you cannot hide anymore. Nowadays, we don't necessarily manifest the origin of our actual names, but we do find ourselves becoming known for the things we've done. Ask anyone who's had the misfortune of having a poor decision go viral on social media. It's a challenge to overcome it! And yet, no human who's even relatively sane wants to be remembered for the worst thing they've ever done. No one wants to be remembered for their unsavory character traits. The gaping holes in our integrity, our flaws and sins, are generally the things we are least proud of.

But the nature of the human condition is that we gravitate toward brokenness. We are drawn to the thing that is the worst about a person. This is partially because we secretly measure ourselves against one another. We say, "Well, at least I didn't do that."

So, like Jacob, too many of us are often forced to introduce ourselves by the things we've done. We lead with our broken places.

"Hi, my name is Adulterer."

"Hey there. Just call me Liar."

"What's up? My name is Thief."

And when this happens, when our past mistakes follow us, everything in our future is at stake. Because what's also true is that no one is saying, "Hey, Thief, come here. I want you to meet my daughter," or "Hey, Liar, come over here. This is your new coworker at the job."

But the beauty of the biblical story of Jacob is that it removes our ability to puff ourselves up and make ourselves look better than someone else based on some arbitrary measurement we've made of their sin against ours. The truth is, we all have something. We may not have the same thing, but we all have *a thing*. My name might be Fear or Shame, and hers might be Insecure, but yours could very well be

Dishonest, Petty, or Myopic. I could go on and on. Everyone has a name that they don't want to be defined by, even if it's something they are still working on not manifesting.

Changing the Narrative

You were taught, with regard to your former way of life, to put off your old self, which is being corrupted by its deceitful desires; to be made new in the attitude of your minds; and to put on the new self, created to be like God in true righteousness and holiness. (Ephesians 4:22–24)

When we filter our old nature through the blood of Jesus Christ, we essentially redefine and reframe our personal narrative. And if we're ever going to be victorious over our old nature and our old flesh, we first have to identify and say what it is. We have to be willing to be honest about our true condition. We must be willing to surround ourselves with authentic relationships, people who will tell us the absolute truth. Our real friends will not only want us to be successful in our careers, they will encourage us to reach for spiritual maturity.

One of the surefire ways to not grow and not change your story—to stay Jacob and never become Israel—is to surround yourself with people who make you comfortable.

The comfort zone is the last place for a name change. In the comfort zone, you get to be what you are and live in "that truth," because "that truth" is subjective. We can pick and choose our truths when we live in a bubble we've carefully crafted. But God's truth does not bend to my personal will. It does not bend to my personal definition.

We all need people who have different lenses and perspectives in our circle: people who will love us enough to tell us the truth, even when we don't want to hear it. At one point in my life, there were things about my character that weren't lining up with the will of God. And there were some people who were bold enough to tell me about myself. I love them for that. I love them for it because they didn't say it to make me feel bad or to shame me; they said it because it didn't line up with the word of God over my life.

You can have a word from God but manifest a name that looks nothing like it. You can manifest the enemy even when God has spoken prophetically over you. Ask Jacob. It's entirely possible to have a carnal name with a godly word. It's representative of our humanity, the battle between flesh and spirit. Jacob was his natural name. Israel was his spiritual name. His mother and father did not give him that second name. His God gave him that name. But he couldn't own it until he went through a process. He had to walk through some things, face the wretchedness of his old identity, in order to manifest the name God gave him.

Diagnosing the Shift

There are a couple of questions we must ask ourselves if we want to identify who we are at our core. These questions help us to examine our actions through the light and lens of the gospel. First, "Does my character line up with the character of Christ?" Second, "Does my heart mirror the heart of Jesus?"

If the answer to either of those is no, we need the proverbial name change.

What does it take to get a name change? I'm not talking about the name your mama gave you. I'm talking about your identity. What does it take to shift your identity into the one God has called you to? Because changing your actual name isn't going to change your behavior, in the same way that putting on makeup isn't going to make you more or less attractive. It's a mask. It covers blemishes and perceived or real flaws. This is an inside job. A shift in identity and character is something that only the Holy Spirit can do. It is the Holy Spirit that changes hearts and lives. Only the Holy Spirit can "change your name," because only the Holy Spirit can change your nature.

What do people say about you? Depending on who you ask, you might have a different name. Sometimes they're incorrect. Sometimes they have ill motives. But then there are those times when those wonderful truth-telling people around you know your real name. Listen to what those folks say as a starting point for diagnosing who you are being called to be.

Once you've allowed the Holy Spirit to speak to you about your character and listened to those in your life who are trustworthy, it's time to face the truth. Be honest in your self-assessment. Consider these questions:

Who am I?

Am I okay with what I've learned about myself?

Is this who I want to be?

Is this who I want to be known as?

Is this what I want to be known for?

There's a hope. Christ in us—that's the hope of glory. In my flesh dwells no good thing. My name might be John, but depending on who has experienced me, my name might be Hurt. My name may represent pain. My name could mean Dismissal. But never forget that our identity can only be found in Christ Jesus. It cannot be outsourced to other people. We can't let other people define us based on what they have gotten from us in the past or what they might get from us in the future. Work on assessing yourself in order to change your actions, but remember that God has defined you from the beginning. He knows who you are and He knows who you'll be.

As I look back over four decades of life, there are so many things I've done wrong, so many places I wish I could go back to. But I can't remain frozen in the moments of my biggest mistakes. Yes, I need to thaw them out and feel them anew, but I also have to move forward. If I freeze the moment, I could end up freezing the process. And we all need the process in order to grow. We need the process to receive our new names. The Bible says, "A good name is to be desired above riches" (see Prov. 22:1).

We need the process to win.

CHAPTER SEVEN

Dreams and Ladders

How often have we been sitting in midst of the divine presence and nature of God and not known it? Have we been so ambitious and so goal oriented that we miss Him? It took a dream on a stone for Jacob to get out of his natural mind and see through his spiritual eyes that God was right there the entire time. It's entirely possible to see God, to identify Him, in those moments when He has manifested Himself in our lives. If we're going to be a victorious church, if we're going to be Christ followers that have real power, real authority, real substance, then we're going to need a move of the Holy Spirit. That move of the spirit requires getting out of our own conventional wisdom, our myopic viewpoints, and our carnal ideas, saying, "God, show me more. Take me higher. And do what You will."

God Exposes Us, Then Uses Us

Let's dig back into this passage that I began discussing in chapter 2. In Genesis 28, we have Jacob on the run and Esau getting married. As he is going from Beersheba to Haran, Jacob falls asleep with a stone under his head. While lying there, he has a dream, a dream of angels ascending and descending a ladder.

This is the place where God spoke to Jacob.

This is the place where Jacob comes face-to-face with his past and his future.

> Jacob left Beersheba and set out for Harran. When he reached a certain place, he stopped for the night because the sun had set. Taking one of the stones there, he put it under his head and lay down to sleep. He had a dream in which he saw a stairway resting on the earth, with its top reaching to heaven, and the angels of God were ascending and descending on it. There above it stood the LORD, and he said: "I am the LORD, the God of your father Abraham and the God of Isaac. I will give you and your descendants the land on which you are lying. Your descendants will be like the dust of the earth, and you will spread out to the west and to the east, to the north and to the south. All peoples on earth will be blessed through you and your offspring. I am with you and will watch

over you wherever you go, and I will bring you back to this land. I will not leave you until I have done what I have promised you." When Jacob awoke from his sleep, he thought, "Surely the LORD is in this place, and I was not aware of it." He was afraid and said, "How awesome is this place! This is none other than the house of God; this is the gate of heaven." (Genesis 28:10–17)

In this moment, Jacob was clearly exhausted in every conceivable way. His ambitions had exposed him. He was emotionally and spiritually naked. This is a place where many of us might find ourselves after spending what seems like a lifetime of manufacturing our success. It's also a place where we will be faced with the opportunity to accept ourselves fully while still holding ourselves accountable.

In other words, it's easy to say, when we are challenged, "Well, this is just me. You need to take it or leave it." Usually in these cases, we learn that people will choose to leave it, and our relationships end up in shambles. God is not necessarily calling us to blow up our relationships out of pride and an unwillingness to be accountable. That said, there is absolutely a way to say, "This is who I am. This is who I am created to be. This is my identity in Christ. And that might be uncomfortable for you. It might even be foreign to you. It might not be what you see for your life, or how you choose to define yourself. But I am well with me, and I'm okay with not being okay with you."

Jacob had not gotten to that place, but he was quickly going to arrive there—beginning that night on the stone.

The Bible says he began to dream, and he saw a ladder stretching from earth to heaven. But the ladder did not originate in the earth, and that is important. The ladder originated from heaven, because angels were ascending and descending on the ladder. What kind of ladder is this, initiated by heaven, reaching the earth? Even as Jacob's prayers were being sent up, God was sending His blessings down. God is simultaneously engaging with us. Whether it's in our dreams, in the silence, or in other unexpected ways, He is always speaking.

The significance of the ladder is that it is symbolic of the partnership between heaven and earth. It is symbolic of the practical and the supernatural. Imagine Jacob, lying on a stone and thinking, "Am I hallucinating? I see angels climbing ladders." And then there is God telling him, "I'm gonna make your descendants as numerous as the sand on the seashore" (see Gen. 22:17). This is the dude that just stole his brother's birthright! This is the guy who has been lying and conniving his whole life! And now God shows up, in the middle of Jacob's dishonesty, in the middle of his usurping of the order of things, and says, "I'm going to bless you."

This is proof that it is never over for us when God is working.

There are many things that should have disqualified Jacob. None of them did. What strikes me is that the providence of God caused God to choose Jacob over Esau before they were even born. Of course, God was able to see ahead and know that Esau's character was not going to line up. We know this by that whole stew debacle. This mama's boy, this little cook at the house, Jacob, was able to manipulate and finesse his brother out of his birthright. He was able to steal Esau's inheritance. Yes, that's awful. It is sinful. And Jacob stayed on the run for it. He paid for it in Laban's house. But Esau was willing to sell his multigenerational blessing for something temporary, and *that* was the character flaw that God saw in Esau's heart.

Once again, allow me some room here. What if Jacob had been praying for God to help him change? What if his heart was pure but his methodology was not? What if his intent was to honor God but he had bad applicable principles? That's like so many of us, right? We have a right heart but wrong execution.

I think the ladder represents the tension that we all feel in our lives, the tension between what heaven said and where we are in the earth. Heaven can declare a thing, but if we don't do our part, it will not come to pass. We must move. We must move on what God has spoken over us. This is the partnership that God is interested in. The mystery of God that we must embrace as believers is that He has chosen our human frailty and condition to be His expressed image. It doesn't make sense to us. But God is sovereign. And amen to Him for being infinitely more wise and powerful than us.

Practical Meets Supernatural

Jacob's ladder is symbolic of the partnership between the practical—what we can do ourselves—and the supernatural—that which only God can do in our lives. It's critical that in every area of our lives—our relationships, businesses, ministries—we are able to marry the practical while maintaining a healthy expectation of the arrival of the supernatural. Until God shows up with His part, we must remain faithful in our part.

Be clear: The ladder was never a figment of Jacob's imagination. It was a real thing. And because he was able to acknowledge and discern it, it became a very special thing. When he woke up, he said, "Surely, I was in the presence of the Lord, and I knew it not" (see Gen. 28:16). Jacob realized that the particular dream he had was not just a function of being tired. God was there. It was Bethel, the house of God. And that's where he built the altar I mentioned earlier.

Sometimes the things we dream about need to become the place where we erect an altar. It needs to be a place where we say, "God, I'm not moving from this dream until I see it come to pass. I anoint the thing I was just sleeping on." For too long, we've been sleeping on our dreams. We've slept on the vision and call of God. Now God is saying, "You need to tell your dream to wake up."

To Dream, We Must Sleep

Another important takeaway from this passage is the significance of sleep, the importance of rest as a precursor to our dreams. I've already talked about the ladder. I've also shared my thoughts on what it means to partner with God. But before we can dream, we must sleep. God is calling some of us to rest. When we rest, we are demonstrating our trust in Him.

As believers, we too often assume that we have to work for the favor of God or work for the miracles of God. But in truth, we couldn't work enough to earn a miracle from God. We can't pray enough prayers. We can't speak in enough tongues or give enough money to earn a miracle. In this season, it's not about earning. The primal position for this next season of your life is the position of rest. I know that this is antithetical to the way Western society achieves. We're a corporate society, and too many of us are constantly climbing the corporate ladder and buying into this dog-eat-dog world where everything is ultracompetitive. And here comes God, saying, "What I'm about to bring to you will not be by your hand or by your effort, it'll be by My power and My spirit and My providence. I simply chose you. It's your time."

When it's your time, there's nothing anybody can do about it. They can whisper and they can wish. They can try to sabotage, but it will not stop the miracle of God or the promise of God from getting to your life—unless *you* stand in the way.

Psalm 63:6 offers us a guide: "When I remember You on my bed, I meditate on You in the night watches" (NAS).

Even while we are sleeping, God's got it under control. He is fixing it in our favor. He is making everything new. As he did with Jacob, God is perfecting that which concerns us. So I encourage you—I encourage myself—to go ahead and rest tonight. Go ahead and smile again. You will win—God's way.

Sleep is more than just rest for your body. It also restores your soul. Most importantly, God wants to show us the power available to us when we rest in Him. Life is always moving at a thousand miles a minute. We've all got tons of responsibilities. But once we grasp the power of rest, we'll realize that rest is a weapon in the hands of a believer. Sin and the trials of life are distractions meant to cause us to lose sight of the fact that God can handle anything we're going through. This is how we become rock solid in our faith. This is how we win.

Sometimes I imagine the Lord's face watching us worry all night. I suspect he's like, "Would they *please* go to bed?! I have it under control. Go to bed! Don't they know I do my best work when they're at rest?"

When we rest, we are essentially saying, "I trust you, God." When we refuse to rest in God, to leave our worries with Him, we end up trying to win in our own way. We try to do things in our own power. Not resting is akin to not having faith.

Have you ever been talking to God and just fallen asleep while you were talking? I'll admit it: I've found myself worried and wondering throughout the night. It's way too easy to sit and stew on our problems. We keep saying to ourselves, *The kids aren't acting right. Our marriage is on the rocks. I don't know how this job thing is gonna work.* But what God wants us to do, as the Psalm alludes to, is to go ahead and meditate on Him. Rest, so we can open ourselves up to the dreams that God wants to show us, the remedies he wants to offer us.

God has the answer. He always does.

There was a time when I was worried about my son. Yes, I know I'm a pastor and I've been preaching over twenty years—which means nothing, because I am human and there's no place where my humanity shows up more than with my children. I had been losing sleep about my son's health and had forgotten one pivotal thing: God knew my boy was going to be facing these issues and He didn't fix it in that moment. He'd ALREADY fixed it long ago. Do you understand what I'm saying? God knew what Jacob would do. He knew the mistakes he would make. But God held the fix from the moment He prophesied purpose over Jacob's life while he was still in the womb. That word God spoke over him hadn't changed. The word that God had spoken over my boy hadn't either.

That's what He wants us to see. Whatever we're dealing

with, God held it years ago. Your answer is just catching up to you; it's been done. God's not struggling to figure out what to do while you are in the middle of a situation. God made it clear in His word that He's always known your story. Isaiah 46:10 says, "I make known the end from the beginning, from ancient times, what is still to come. I say, 'My purpose will stand, and I will do all that I please.'"

In my case, God knew that John IV was going to have some breathing issues, so he orchestrated my boy's healing, beginning all the way back on December 15 of 1981. That is the day my wife, Aventer Cotton, was born. God implanted into that baby girl turned adolescent turned teen turned young woman a passion and a desire to learn about lungs and breathing and cardiopulmonary science. He opened the doors for her to get degrees in these fields, all so that when she gave birth to our legacy, she would be able to identify the attack of the enemy in a way that maybe another mother wouldn't—and tell the doctors what they need to do. God had it all under control. But he needed us to rest, and trust that He had it all worked out.

God is never caught off guard by any situation that occurs in our lives. He has handled it all. Jesus can see something dead and pronounce it only sleep. Don't believe me? Ask Luke.

But when Jesus heard it, He answered him, saying, "Do not be afraid; only believe, and she will be made well." When He came into the house, He permitted no one to go in except Peter, James, and John, and the father and mother of the girl. Now all wept and mourned for her; but He said, "Do not weep; she is not dead, but sleeping." And they ridiculed Him, knowing that she was dead.

But He put them all outside, took her by the hand and called, saying, "Little girl, arise." Then her spirit returned, and she arose immediately. And He commanded that she be given something to eat. (See Luke 8:50–55)

You think your situation is dead, but Jesus declared it's just sleep. Which means the moment the word left His mouth, it was looking for you. God is speaking something with your name on it, and it's looking for you. Sadly, for some of us, the healing word of Christ can't get to us because the stone of condemnation and shame is in the way. Some of us are so ashamed of our past that we feel we don't deserve the blessing of God.

Sure, by the law, what we have done should have cost us all our destinies. It should thwart our purposes. But by the power of grace, Jesus says, "I'm removing the law and I'm giving you what you don't deserve and what you could not earn."

So even though my son's body, based on the fallen state of humanity, was not functioning properly, his body did not have the final say. Jesus was speaking to his little body and saying "Live!" Life was declared even though he wasn't breathing. Jesus was like, "Yeah, this sickness is not unto death but for the glory of God that the Son of God might be glorified" (see John 11:4).

Again, God has it all under control for you. He has a dream He wants to show you. Something He planned long ago. But you need to rest. Like Jacob, you need to go to sleep. Jesus speaks to what we call dead. It doesn't matter what state your past or present is in. Jesus has just spoken to it, and even though you may still have some things in bondage, God is sending people to free you, to loose you and let you go.

Have you ever felt the presence of God while you were sleeping?

There are times when my little buddy, IV, or my daughter, Theory, will be sleeping in their room and my wife and I will go to tuck them in. We'll make sure that their feet are under the cover. Sometimes I'll lightly kiss them on the forehead. In those moments, I realize just how much I love them. They don't realize it, but we are there loving them deeply even while they are asleep. We are preparing them for their next day, their next encounter. Packing their lunches for the following day and putting crackers in their snacks. Getting their clothes laid out. They don't have a clue, but it's all being worked out for them. That's just like God. He knows you've been struggling and he sees you sleep. He is there. Present. Loving you. Preparing the next day, the next encounter. He is saying, "I have a plan for your life. I already got it worked out. I just need you to sleep tonight, baby. Daddy's got it under control."

As with Jacob, God definitely is waiting to speak to you, even in your sleep. He wants you to rest in Him, and as you do so, He will reveal some things to you. But God isn't just speaking, He's sowing.

Sowing While You Sleep

Gen. 2:7–8 says, "And the LORD God formed man *of* the dust of the ground, and breathed into his nostrils the breath of life; and man became a living soul. And the LORD God planted a garden eastward in Eden; and there he put the man whom he had formed" (KJV).

Let's think about this: God created Adam, then he went and planted a garden. God was sowing. He put something in the garden and then went and got the man he had formed and put him in the garden.

While we are sleeping, God is sowing. He is preparing you and everything connected to you for the next level of your destiny. God is about to surprise us. He knows we think that His presence is enough—and it is. But He wants to place us, like Adam, in our own proverbial garden. He wants to give us a purpose. He wants us in a fruitful place. He wants to put us in a position to win—His way.

Life is not always going to be tears and sadness and

thorns, and broken dreams and hearts. While we rest, God is sowing good things into the ground, and he's going to bring us into the planting that he has purposed for our lives.

Make a Demand on Heaven

Here's what I believe. I believe that if we have the boldness to speak and to declare certain things, heaven must respond. We don't get to determine what that response is or the form it will take, but God will answer. One of the ways heaven responds is by sending us angels. Psalm 91:11–12 says, "He will command his angels concerning you to guard you in all your ways; they will lift you up in their hands, so that you will not strike your foot against a stone."

The ladder is an eternal initiation with an earthly manifestation.

So just imagine this: the moment you start speaking and declaring your needs and the God-given desires of your heart (see Ps. 27:4), your angels start moving up your ladder to get the thing you've been praying for and bring it back down. What if you have a "heavier" angel because you haven't been talking to God enough? What if your angel's legs and arms are atrophied from lack of use? What if your angel has cobwebs on their wings from not having to navigate the winds between earth and heaven? What if God wants to do something monumental and worldwide with you? Not the other person. Not someone down the street. What if it's you? What if it's me? To win in God's economy might mean we need to dream bigger. Embrace the fact that God speaks to us. He has given us dreams, and if we go by what He demonstrated to Jacob, that means there's something He wants to bring down to our realm.

CHAPTER EIGHT

Pot Meet Kettle

Jacob's father-in-law, Laban, was more tricky and conniving than Jacob could ever dream of being. It's recorded in Scripture that Laban cheated Jacob out of wages. In line with the title of this chapter, Jacob was the *Pot* that finally met his *Kettle* in Laban. And on the journey to winning in the way God intended, he learned the hard way that there is always someone who is smarter and trickier than us. God will often allow you to meet somebody or to come into the presence of people who are like you in negative ways, because too often that's the only way we can see those negative attributes in ourselves.

God's love is so vast that He is patient with us and He allows us to walk through years of failure and bad decisions. As a loving father, He does this in order to cause us to have to come to grips with those areas of ourselves that need to go away or be checked. If we're going to win in the areas that matter most—with our family, in the area of personal accountability, at work, and in our commitment to build the Kingdom of God—then He must address the areas that have been corrupted by desire or unchecked ambition. God allowed Jacob to run right into the house of Laban, not just so he could marry his daughters, but so that Jacob could see what he would become if he did not address his character issues. By putting us in contact with a future version of ourselves, sometimes He enables us to see what we should never desire to become.

See Yourself in Them

Sometimes the hardest person to see is ourselves. Part of God's development of us as winners, if we are willing to accept the process, is to reveal our true character through the people around us. This course of development is not designed to shame or humiliate us, but it is to admonish us to engage and integrate whatever is necessary to remove what shouldn't have been there in the first place.

I don't have to look very far to find cautionary tales of what not to do as a man. Unfortunately, the lineage of men in my family has been wrought with challenges and tragedy. I saw relational failure all around me. Absent fathers were common. Guys who ran from their challenges and who skirted the issues were the regulars in my childhood. These men would have been more effective men—not perfect, but certainly more fruit bearing—had they embraced those necessary places in their lives and chosen to deal with and heal from their own pain.

And here I am, seeing a trait here and there of my uncles in my own heart and terrified of becoming one of them. I'm terrified of ending up back in my mother's house, talking about who I *almost* was, what I could've or should've been, or what I used to be.

What Laban represents is God introducing Jacob to himself from the outside, but also showing Jacob a glimpse of his future if he didn't change.

What's Good for the Goose...

So Laban brought together all the people of the place and gave a feast. But when evening came, he took his daughter Leah and brought her to Jacob, and Jacob made love to her. And Laban gave his servant Zilpah to his daughter as her attendant. When morning came, there was Leah! So Jacob said to Laban, "What is this you have done to me? I served you for Rachel, didn't I? Why have you deceived me?" Laban replied, "It is not our custom here to give the younger daughter in marriage before the older one. Finish this daughter's bridal week; then we will give you the younger one also, in return for another seven years of work." And Jacob did so. He finished the week with

Leah, and then Laban gave him his daughter Rachel to be his wife. Laban gave his servant Bilhah to his daughter Rachel as her attendant. Jacob made love to Rachel also, and his love for Rachel was greater than his love for Leah. And he worked for Laban another seven years. (Genesis 29:22–30)

Laban realized that Jacob was not in a power position, so he took Jacob's vulnerability and manipulated it for his own gain. Sound familiar, Jacob? It's clear that Jacob was reaping what he'd sown in his relationship with his brother, Esau. Many times when people say, "You'll reap what you sow," they think that what you've done to somebody else will happen exactly that way to you. I don't always believe that. The truth is, if we're doing things to purposely hurt someone, God has a way of dealing with us. And those consequences will not always be meted out in ways we can anticipate.

In fact, the principle of reaping what you've sown (see Gal. 6:9) rarely shows up in the form we think it will. Sure, if it wasn't for God's grace and mercy, we'd all be consumed by the wrong things we've done and thought. We've all made bad decisions. But if we live a life where we consistently sow one thing, we cannot be surprised when we harvest that thing.

I look at my life and there have been moments when I have sown great seed. I have done what I believe are noble things. But there are also moments when I've done horrible

things, things I wish I could take back. I'm ashamed of
them. I'm disgusted by them. And there were times when I
had to pay for what I'd done.

But the redemption in all of this is that good and bad
seed become crops that are raised together. And there were
many times when I just knew that judgment was coming, but it was grace that showed up. It was almost like the
mercy of God and the grace of God kind of intertwined
and interlocked, and canceled each other out.

But God does not deal in cheap grace. What generally
happens is, the areas where we are supposed to progress can
end up being canceled out by the negative seed we've sown.
And in the areas where I should have been easily consumed
by my sins, that consummation was canceled out by some
of the good seed I'd sown.

The thing is, we don't get to choose when either is going
to happen. God does. And because of that, we must keep
sowing good seed in the direction we are called to go.

The Big Payback

Jacob sowed many seeds of deception. Driven by his
unchecked ambition, he'd exploited vulnerability for his
own gain. He'd finally come to a moment in his life when
he was lonely, disconnected from his family, and utterly
exposed by God. Enter: Laban. Laban is his uncle and

the father of the woman he's fallen in love with—Rachel. Lonely, in love, and without family has to be the epitome of what it means to be in a vulnerable place.

Laban sees this guy's willing to do whatever it takes for Rachel, and so he capitalizes on that vulnerability. Just as Jacob saw Esau's hunger, Laban sees Jacob's hunger and sets him up.

God will show us that we can change, although He is not beyond doing it in a way that startles. But if you are willing to learn the lessons, endure the tests, and embrace what God is showing you, you can change. You can become something different. God never shows you who you are through the actions of another just for observational purposes. He wants these experiences to be transformational. That's why He allows it.

Spots and Freckles

So, as we see, God will show us ourselves by showing us exactly what we will become if we continue to not walk in integrity. The root word of *integrity* is *integer*, which means "whole number." Too many of us are only a fraction of ourselves because we have been beaten down by life or we have been the victim of a myriad of tragedies—self-inflicted or otherwise. And all too often, in the process of dealing with the trauma we've endured, we become just like the thing we despise. Living victorious means being able to see the broken without letting it overtake you to the extent that your character is compromised.

After Rachel had had Joseph, Jacob spoke to Laban, "Let me go back home. Give me my wives and children for whom I've served you. You know how hard I've worked for you."

Laban said, "If you please, I have learned through divine inquiry that God has blessed me because of you." He went on, "So name your wages. I'll pay you."

Jacob replied, "You know well what my work has meant to you and how your livestock has flourished under my care. The little you had when I arrived has increased greatly; everything I did resulted in blessings for you. Isn't it about time that I do something for my own family?"

"So, what should I pay you?"

Jacob said, "You don't have to pay me a thing. But how about this? I will go back to pasture and care for your flocks. Go through your entire flock today and take out every speckled or spotted sheep, every dark-colored lamb, every spotted or speckled goat. They will be my wages. That way you can check on my honesty when you assess my wages. If you find any goat that's not speckled or spotted or a sheep that's not black, you will know that I stole it."

"Fair enough," said Laban. "It's a deal."

But that very day Laban removed all the mottled and spotted billy goats and all the speckled and spotted nanny goats, every animal that had even a touch of white on it plus all the black sheep and placed them under the care of his sons. Then he put a three-day journey between himself and Jacob. Meanwhile Jacob went on tending what was left of Laban's flock.

But Jacob got fresh branches from poplar, almond, and plane trees and peeled the bark, leaving white stripes on them. He stuck the peeled branches in front of the watering troughs where the flocks came to drink. When the flocks were in heat, they came to drink and mated in front of the streaked branches. Then they gave birth to young that were streaked or spotted or speckled. Jacob placed the ewes before the dark-colored animals of Laban. That way he got distinctive flocks for himself which he didn't mix with Laban's flocks. And when the sturdier animals were mating, Jacob placed branches at the troughs in view of the animals so that they mated in front of the branches. But he wouldn't set up the branches before the feebler animals. That way the feeble animals went to Laban and the sturdy ones to Jacob. The man got richer and richer, acquiring huge flocks, lots and lots of servants, not to mention camels and donkeys. (Genesis 30: 25–43 MSG)

Jacob was being tricked by his father-in-law and, in turn, decided to use his wits against the man. In the process of breeding lambs and goats, he made a deal with Laban that said his father-in-law could keep the cattle that were born with pure white fur and he'd keep the spotted animals since they were viewed as less valuable. Laban attempted to trick Jacob once more by removing any lamb or goat that would likely produce others with spots or freckles—but Jacob found a way to breed the animals in his favor.

There are several interpretations of this account. Many of us might ask, Why did Jacob ask for this deal? Was this just another form of manipulation on his part? Or was this a way for him to show Laban that he was not the same man who had entered his house? I'd venture to say the latter.

The spotted cattle were ultimately utilized by Jacob to give himself the best advantage—but only because he'd righted himself before God. We too can use our spots and freckles to improve ourselves. If we are wise and work toward standing righteous before God, our spots and freckles will not become places of shame or minimized value; they will be places of destiny.

Mirror, Mirror

Jacob's experience in Laban's house was about self-discovery. It taught him not only that there are consequences for his actions, it also showed him who he didn't want to be and how hard he was willing to work to make things right. In a nutshell, his journey showed him exactly who he was in a way he'd never seen before.

Do you know who you are? If not, God will use the circumstances of your life to show you.

We all have moments of painful self-discovery. It's part of the process. For me, there have been some painful places I've had to explore even in the writing of this book, and if it wasn't for this particular season of my life, I would not have accepted it. I would've rejected the lessons and, in doing so, been lost. So what I've come to realize is that when God reveals who you are through the painful place, it's actually His love at work. God is saying, "Let Me show you who you are. Let Me tell you who you are." He's ready to our truth.

Laban was Jacob's first mirror. I've had my own mirrors and you will certainly have yours. The mirror shows you who you are. And until you see it, the reflection will continue to shine back on you all that God wants to perfect. But, thank the Lord, there does come a moment of shattering. This is when the image in the mirror is not acceptable to you. This is when you finally decide that you have the power to change.

Getting to Self-Discovery

We often hear church folks crying out about how the church is "moving too far from holiness." And maybe there is some truth about that. But what is often not talked about is the fact that holiness is not always about what "they" aren't doing "over there." Holiness is nothing more than personal responsibility for the faith that we say we believe in. Holiness doesn't come from our willpower. Holiness is birthed from a real relational encounter with God. He empowers you to make wise decisions. But it's still up to us to walk in that power. Free will affords us the ability to do what we want. It also affords us the consequences for those actions.

Imagine how Jacob felt when he woke up and realized that he'd lain in covenant with someone he didn't want and hadn't worked for. Laban had stolen from him. I can imagine Jacob crying and pleading for His blessing, saying, "Father, can you believe this dude did this to me?! God, this is crazy!"

And God saying, "Yeah. Does it remind you of anybody?"

And Jacob saying, "No. Not at all. That's crazy. I would never do that to someone. That doesn't make any sense."

Sometimes we don't always get it the first time around.

Since he didn't get the lesson, maybe he needed seven more years. Maybe he needed more time to reflect. Maybe he needed more time to see himself.

I know for sure that God will keep you in the process until you see what you need to see about yourself. There have been so many times I've gone to God about my marriage and said, "You need to deal with Aventer." And He was like, "Why don't you tell me about you?" And I'm like, "No. I'm good. I'm amazing." And the truth? Well, the truth was, I'm very far from amazing. I'm quite belligerent with my words when I get angry, and I can be very hostile. I also shut down and become unemotional when faced with a relational exchange necessary for healthy and vital marital peace.

What I'm now learning to do when I get angry is to pause and ask God, "What is that?" Nine times out of ten, God is like, "Mirror." Then there's an opportunity for me to check myself. But here's the thing: you can't see yourself in a mirror unless you're close to it. And so it is God's way to make the relationships that are closest to you the ones most likely to show you who you are. Every time I've gotten frustrated with Aventer, I can absolutely identify something in me that reminds me of that moment. So the challenge is: If God is using my wife to show me myself, how many other times has he tried to get my attention but I've either ignored it, missed it, or couldn't discern it?

Jacob learned what I have learned and what we all must learn at some point: the process of getting to the truth about who we are, even about who God is, often goes through people. We often want to reach up to God and skip all the lessons wrapped in flesh He's sent our way. God will allow you to see some things before you even get up to Him. We want to be closer to God. We say, "God, I want to see you. I want to know you." And I imagine God is like, "That's a wonderful and noble thing, but in My presence there is absolute truth. And so nothing that is a lie can exist in here with Me, even if it's a lie you don't know you're living."

So He helps us.

He says, "Let Me help you as you get closer to Me. Let Me show you who you are. Let Me do this so you're not shocked or overwhelmed at how I deal with you." Because generally, the only one who doesn't know who I am is me. The only one who doesn't know who you are, Dear Reader, is you. God is not shocked by anything we've ever done. He knew it was there. He knows our motivations even when we don't.

The Blessing Isn't Going Anywhere

Here is what's interesting: Jacob had the blessing of his father, illegally stolen from his brother, but he had no power over his uncle in that whole situation. He was still subjected to the pain and deceit wielded by Laban. So you got a word from God? You got a blessing that's been prophesied over you? Great! But to truly win God's way, you are going to have to walk through seasons of submission, testing, proving, and serving. It's going to look like you are losing for a while before the win shows up.

The very thing that Jacob had run from his whole life was now what he had to embrace. He now had to work for what he wanted. He had to endure unfairness. He had to feel unsafe for a long time. And that's often our story. Our blessing hasn't gone anywhere. But we do have to get comfortable with being uncomfortable to get to it. Sitting in safety and the confines of what is familiar will not get you your win. Jacob would never have become Israel had he not met Laban. Laban was essential to Jacob's journey toward self-awareness and identity.

CHAPTER NINE

Face-to-Face

The time had come. Jacob was going to have to face his brother, Esau. More than that, he was going to have to face his past. And ultimately, he was going to have to face God. Jacob had lived a little bit since he'd run off nearly twenty years prior. He'd seen some things. He'd learned what it means to reap what you sow. And the Bible says he was willing to do whatever it took to reconcile. As Esau approached, Jacob sent his two wives, his sons, maidservants, all that he had, to Jabbok. Jabbok is Hebrew for *emptying*. God was requiring Jacob to empty himself of everything that he had accumulated, all of his ambition, all of his lies—everything he had amassed.

No more running, Jacob. God was about to make clear the point that He'd been dropping like breadcrumbs throughout Jacob's life. It's the message he's been giving us throughout this book. The way to win is to lose. Jacob was about to win his identity and his purpose—this time legitimately.

Settle Your Debts

Then Jacob prayed, "O God of my father Abraham, God of my father Isaac, LORD, you who said to me, 'Go back to your country and your relatives, and I will make you prosper,' I am unworthy of all the kindness and faithfulness you have shown your servant. I had only my staff when I crossed this Jordan, but now I have become two camps. Save me, I pray, from the hand of my brother Esau, for I am afraid he will come and attack me, and also the mothers with their children. But you have said, 'I will surely make you prosper and will make your descendants like the sand of the sea, which cannot be counted.'" (Genesis 32: 9–12)

After leaving Laban, Jacob had acquired everything a man could want. He'd built a family and amassed great wealth. He held the birthright and had been blessed by his father. But Jacob had yet to address how he got it. God is not going to settle you until you settle your debts. You want credit, Jacob? That's what your prayer indicates. Well, if you want credit, settle your debts.

I know it's easy to forget the stuff in the middle. We see the prophecy over Jacob's life and say, "Well, God chose him from the beginning." We see the twelve sons and all the livestock. None of that changes the fact that he stole something. It just means that God was going to use him even though he stole it.

And this brings up all kinds of morality clauses and questions about whether God preordained for Jacob to steal Esau's blessing or if God foresaw that Jacob would steal Esau's blessing and, because of the character of Jacob versus the character of Esau, made a decision that would lead us to Jesus. Whatever position you take, at the end of the day this is not about absolving Jacob of the clear wrong. It's about what happens after a wrong has occurred. How do we reconcile our wrongs?

Jacob had been running a long time when he reached Jabbok. It was time. Whether as a strategy or as a form of repentance, he sent everything he had away, and then he sat with himself. For the first time in a long while, he was alone. He didn't have just one wife, he had two. He didn't have just one kid, he had eleven. He didn't just have a couple of sheep, he had a flock. He didn't have one assistant, he had a staff of maidservants and menservants. He'd amassed all of this but had never addressed himself or his origin. It was time to face it.

When Your Origin Calls

[Jacob] spent the night there, and from what he had with him he selected a gift for his brother Esau: two hundred female goats and twenty male goats, two hundred ewes and twenty rams, thirty female camels with their young, forty cows and ten bulls, and twenty female donkeys and ten male donkeys. He put them in the care of his servants, each herd by itself, and said to his servants, "Go ahead of me, and keep some space between the herds."

He instructed the one in the lead: "When my brother Esau meets you and asks, 'Who do you belong to, and where are you going, and who owns all these animals in front of you?' then you are to say, 'They belong to your servant Jacob. They are a gift sent to my lord Esau, and he is coming behind us.'" (Genesis 32:13–18)

Esau was coming. His presence was going to be a reminder to Jacob of everything that had transpired before. Jacob had to finally prepare for confrontation, and what does he do? He sends gifts. Esau was coming to see him and Jacob said, "Let me just send gift after gift to appease him." He essentially was trying to buy his way out of getting killed. He wanted to use his gifts to get out of confrontation.

Jacob and John, together again.

If I'm honest, I've also used the skill set of charisma or charm to sidestep process. My whole life is a testimony to what I haven't faced. There have been many times when I have wanted my life to end, not necessarily because outwardly life was so bad, but because I would rather not face the responsibility of dealing with those areas in my life that are uncomfortable.

Like many men I've met, I'd rather die with the perception of being heroic than live and do the hard work of becoming a man. And at every turn, God has forced me to do exactly that: the work. I often joke that I'm the kind of dude that if I jumped off a building, I'd probably only break my legs or something, because God is not going to let me die a fake hero. When I die, I'll die a real man—a man who finally faced all he ever was.

No Escape

Jacob was a slippery guy. He was always able to slip free even if it was only by a hair. He barely escaped Esau and, with the help of Rebekah, got out of the house just in time. And while he had to work, he eventually escaped his father-in-law (see Gen. 31). Jacob did whatever it took to not face a thing. He got what he needed or wanted and kept it moving.

But what Jacob didn't realize was that God's will to turn

him around lived in all his accumulation. See, there comes a point when you have so much that it becomes no longer as easy to run. Jacob couldn't run as fast with wives and children and others he was responsible for. And even if he tried to run, he wasn't going to get too far. The past becomes increasingly difficult to ignore, no matter how cool you play it.

Oh, He's Coming

We lie to ourselves.

We lie to God.

We say, "I'm cool. God's cool with me." But then we read His word and stare into the reflections provided by the "mirrors" He sends our way, and nothing about our character looks like His word.

Sometimes we are fooled because, for a season, our gifts are working. God is using our gifts so we believe that He is okay with what we've been doing. Time will pass, and we'll make the mistake of thinking that our Esau isn't coming. We somehow believe we have escaped God's discipline. We think that because we are [fill in your gift/talent/ability here] and He hasn't confronted us, that He will never confront us. That's foolish. That's making a mockery of God's grace—cheapening it.

The time lapse that can sometimes occur between your past and your confrontation is actually the presence of God's grace. It's God saying, "I'm giving you a chance."

Just like Jacob's, your past will likely confront you in your present before you ever can truly put your hands on the future. I know this for sure. Everything I've ever done points back to my beginnings in ministry. It points back to being a single youth pastor in New Jersey, starting a ministry called MannaGod and touring the stage play *The Journey*. It points back to me, sleeping on my business partner Glenn's couch while I worked on records. And so much of that pointing back—the mistakes I made during that time period—is now pointing to my present.

I wrote and recorded an R & B album titled *Covenant* and a gospel album titled *Journey*. At the time, I was clear that I had no hope of being some sexy R & B artist, so in turn, I wrote an entire album based off what I thought love was. Unfortunately, it was an ideal that was far from the reality of what it takes to make love work. Writing that album messed me up, because I started looking for somebody to fit those songs.

The songs are beautiful. But the songs have no human attached to them. They are just the imaginings of a lonely young man who, like everyone else, had been influenced by the false images of love and relationships found in the media. In my mind, there was somebody perfect out there for me. I was basically looking for Jesus in the form of a woman, a perfect human being that can save me from myself. This is why my marriage was doomed to fail if I didn't course-correct. Aventer's last name was not Christ, and I was trying too hard to make her a god.

When I couldn't worship her, and when I realized that she couldn't save me, there was a part of me—a part I'm deeply ashamed of—that felt like I had no use for her. I despised her in my heart because in my mind I had set up that she would be the one that could save me from the past.

I think the profound sense of loneliness I felt contributed to the suffering in my marriage. I found myself longing for a place of deep connection, and when my wife, who's eight and a half years younger than me, could not provide it, I secretly began blaming her, saying to her in many not uncertain terms, "You're not giving me what I need." But I had not gone to God. I had ceased to be the priest, the protector and the provider of my home, and I was angry that my wife wasn't leading. I blamed her for not being me, for not getting me out of the funk that I was in. I put so much responsibility on her because I refused to face myself and the role I was playing in her pain.

In some of the same ways, Jacob during his time with Laban decided, "I love Rachel. No, I don't even know her, but I love her. She's it!" (see Gen. 29). He resisted what I imagine to be God's whisper: "Leah's the one who can give you an heir."

Jacob, much like me, likely responded with, "I don't want that, God. I want what I want. I want what looks good. I want what I had in my mind." And as God is wont to do, He made Jacob face the truth. He gave him Leah first because the fantasy of Rachel actually brought a reality of barrenness.

This idea that God will make you face a thing is powerful and life changing if you let it transform you. God's all-encompassing love forces those of us who desire to be truly victorious to win according to His word. And that entails losing—losing your pride, will, ego, and ultimately yourself.

He Wants It All

We have to be willing to lose it all. As we've covered here, Jacob was one wrestling match from internal victory. For any contest, there's usually a fee attached. In Jacob's case, he had to pay it all. God said, "Give me everything before you cross over into reconciliation and purpose. I want it all. Give me your wives, your kids, your money, your future, your ability to earn income. I want it all."

This is a deep prophetic glimpse into what Jesus says later in Scripture:

> If anyone comes to me and does not hate father and mother, wife and children, brothers and sisters—yes, even their own life—such a person cannot be my disciple. (Luke 14:26)

Jesus is saying, "I want it all. Nothing less than everything." We tend to wrestle with what we think is of value in our lives, and God is saying, "Nothing is! What's most valuable is in My presence." And what we learn is that nothing we want, nothing we think will make us winners, will be accessible if we make gods out of them.

The imagery of giving up our all and surrendering to God is never clearer than in what happens after Jacob sends all his things ahead to Esau or away from danger. We've previously talked about the altar Jacob created and his wrestling match with God, but I think I want to do a deep dive in that text one final time.

> So Jacob was left alone, and a man wrestled with him
> till daybreak. (Genesis 32:24)

Let's be clear: Jacob wasn't trying to build a nation. He was trying to find a comfortable bubble, a safe place where he could worship the world he'd created. And God said, "No, we're going to have to wrestle. We're going to have to talk about this. You're going to have to face Me because I'm not going to let you worship at the altar of what you think you've amassed or accumulated. You will not worship at the altar of things."

Let me grab some more of that leeway here. What God was saying to Jacob and what I believe He is saying to us is: "There's a word over your life, so you will not worship at the altar of your accomplishments. You will not worship at the altar of self-congratulation and the applause of people. You will not worship at the altar of your gift and how people elevate your gift. You're going to face Me, but before you do, give Me everything that's in your hands. Give Me all of that."

Jacob was left alone, and it was at night. Think about that. There's no place to run. He doesn't know if Esau's going to say *nah* to his gifts and creep up and kill him. But somehow he knows that he can't run anymore. I suppose he could have physically run, but I suspect that, after all Jacob had been through, he'd finally got to the point where he was tired of running.

God does that, you know. God will let us stay on the hamster wheel of achievement for a good minute. He will let us run ourselves ragged until we decide to get off and come and take a long drink of His living water. Then He brings us to a point of complete submission by setting us apart from everything we hold dear. Especially in this day and age, it's entirely too easy to keep the noise going. We stay distracted, sometimes intentionally, so that we are unable to sit with ourselves and hear the voice of God. And then God allows a situation to occur where the stillness is our only option.

So many preachers and pastors like myself struggle with this very thing. Maybe teachers and engineers do too. For the better part of my ministry, all I've done is run. Thinking I'm going somewhere but going nowhere. Like a hamster, I run in that circle over and over and, in the places that really matter, make no moves. Yes, I go get a little bit of water. When I'm thirsty, I go grab a little bit of His word. But then I go back to running. I'm never still long enough to take in enough word to satisfy my thirst. I only take in enough to satisfy the thirst of the people I'm preaching to. So instead of becoming stronger in the word for my own healing, I'm just a conduit. And after a while, that can turn you bitter.

I became bitter and angry. I wonder if Jacob did too. I imagine he was tired and said, "You know what? Whatever's coming, I'm going to face it. It may cost me my life, but I'm so tired of running. I might get punched, but I'm punching back."

Empty or Full of It?

God essentially told Jacob, "You can't face me until you're empty." Why? Why did Jacob have to give up everything, material and otherwise?

God is not going to introduce Himself to you when you're so full of…well, you. He won't face you, and he won't let you face Him. Anybody who's full of themselves cannot be filled by the spirit of God. That's why Jacob had to be empty. That's why we must face God and ourselves empty.

In the middle of the desert, Jacob began to fight. Scripture doesn't exactly give details of the fight, but he was wrestling, so I'm sure his heartbeat was elevated and there were probably plenty of tears. Jacob was ready and willing to die. He was tired.

I get that.

One of the questions I've gotten quite a bit is this: "What's wrong, John?" My answer is nearly always, "I'm tired." Or I'm asked, "Are you sleepy?" And of course, my answer is the same: "No, I'm tired." Running in search of what I thought was success but having absolutely no peace was exhausting. Having acclaim and popularity but no joy or healthy substantive relationships was taxing on the soul.

It's the love of God that says, "All right, John. You've looked for My face in everybody else. You've worshiped at the altar of your accomplishments and achievements. Your wife and kids can't save you. Your position at Lakewood can't save you. Your new church can't save you. Your worship team can't save you. No one can save you—but Me. You're going to have to face Me."

And that's exactly what happened.

I was getting ready to preach at Lakewood and had a couple of the men who are going to move their families to Greenville to serve with me in the ministry God called me to pastor. They said, "Let us pray for our pastor."

[Sidebar: It's still so weird that they call me pastor. I don't feel like a pastor. Most days, I feel like a failure. I feel like the wizard behind the curtain. In that way, Jacob and I are very much alike.]

So they were praying for me and I hear God say in my spirit, "I'm not listening to them." It was almost like I could physically see God batting their prayers away from His throne. In my imagination, God wasn't looking at anybody else in that room. He was looking at me. He was looking at me, because He knew what I knew. I knew that I didn't want to face Him. I was willing to let them pray for me because maybe then God would be so distracted by their prayers that He wouldn't see that I don't want to deal. Of course, God says, "I know you better than you know yourself, and since you won't do what you need to do, I'm going to have to come put my hands on you." And that's what He did. Everything changed from that point.

When God has invested a great deal into a person, He will engage them. Jacob couldn't go up to wrestle with God, so God came down to wrestle with him. What a loving God we have that He will come to our level and engage us where we are. He will put His hands on us in our immaturity, fear, insecurity, and brokenness, and wrestle with us all night.

Leaders Who Limp

Then the man said, "Let me go, for it is daybreak." But Jacob replied, "I will not let you go unless you bless me." (Genesis 32:26)

The angel of the Lord said, "Let me go." Now, in truth, God could have snapped Jacob's neck, but instead He'd only touched the socket of Jacob's hip. You can't pivot with bad hips. You can't change direction.

Bo Jackson was a Hall of Fame baseball player and football player whose hip popped out in a game against the Cincinnati Bengals. Somebody grabbed the bottom of his leg, and because he was built with such force in his thighs and his hips, even though his leg was planted, his hips kept going. Jackson was never the same again. God didn't snap Jacob's neck to paralyze him. He just made it so he would limp. And that's exactly what God wants: leaders who limp. Because when you face God, you become acutely aware of your deficiencies. That's a good thing for leaders to know in order to keep the flesh and ego in check.

When we face God, we see our limitations. Our limp is our greatest reminder of our inability to do anything of value on our own. There comes a point in time when our physical human ability comes to its end, when what we know how to do meets its limit. And at that moment, when we have exhausted our resources and stretched ourselves to the breaking point, God says, "I got it." And when God emerges, He shows you who He is. God produces glory in such a profound way. But the key is to allow God to do it and for us to stay in our position.

That's hard.

Really hard.

We recognize that we are helpless without God, that we can do nothing without Him. There is no victory, no chance, and no hope without God. And that's okay, because

God is actively pursuing those of us who have come to this point. He's not a bad cop, policing our every move so He can punish us. God desires reconciliation. He desires our rehabilitation. And He knows that only He has the tools to help us return back to His purpose and be better people.

We often think victory comes with hard work and perseverance. Those are important traits to have, but no, victory is from the Lord. Jacob was face-to-face with the King of glory, and even after God shrunk his hip, he wouldn't let go. Jacob had been running his whole life, and he was willing to fight all night. He wrestled all night, and even though he knew he couldn't win, he said, "I ain't going to let go, because whatever this is, I want it to bless me."

The wrestling we experience as we come face-to-face with God brings about a realization that we are actually in a moment of miraculous designation. It feels like a wrestling match, but it's actually a manifestation of a blessing. How did the angel of the Lord manifest the blessing? By giving Jacob a name change.

Telling the Truth

Let's revisit Jacob's wrestling match for one moment. Genesis 32:26–28 says:

> Then the man said, "Let me go, for it is daybreak."
> But Jacob replied, "I will not let you go unless you

bless me." The man asked him, "What is your name?" "Jacob," he answered. Then the man said, "Your name will no longer be Jacob, but Israel, because you have struggled with God and with humans and have overcome."

What is fascinating about the exchange between Jacob and the One he wrestles is that it signifies both the culminating point of one aspect of his life and the originating point of another. Two lives, one man. In one moment, there is death and life; an end and a beginning; the end of time and the beginning of eternity.

In the course of the wrestling match, God put his hands on Jacob's hip. I suspect that he wanted all people to be reminded that whatever He touches has to change. It can never go back to what it was. It could never be the same. Jacob lived with a limp for the rest of his life.

It's also striking that God asks a man his name. Among all the characteristics of God, there is omniscience. He knows all things. And of course He does, because He is the creator and originator of all things. So He didn't ask Jacob his name because He didn't know it. He asked because He wanted to know if Jacob knew it.

Jacob had been running from his true identity for the entirety of his life. Therefore, God was essentially asking, "What do you answer to? What have you been known as? What do people call you? Finally, who are you? Have you come to grips with the truth of your condition?" God cannot help what we do not face. Jacob wasn't wrestling for a blessing, he was wrestling for an identity he didn't know he had. That may be why God didn't ask him, "How do you feel?" He didn't ask him, "What do you want?" He went straight for the jugular: "Who are you?"

How profound is that? Inside of Jacob's simple response was the answer that God was looking for. God essentially wanted to ask him, "Do you know that you are enough as Jacob for me to come and see about you?" For so long, people have had this idea that God is so holy that He doesn't touch broken things. And yet Jacob was very much a broken man. Just like most of us. We are broken individuals. That is the beauty of the community we call the church. We are broken, but we are broken together. When I was growing up at the Bethel Baptist Church in Cincinnati, we had stained-glass windows on both sides of our sanctuary, and the beauty of these images was made more poignant when the light from the sun would reflect into the sanctuary. These different colored pieces of glass connected to create one picture. That is the nature of the church. We are all broken pieces of glass stitched together to create a picture of God's glory. But we cannot accurately reflect the light of Christ or refract the love of God unless we come to grips with our true identity. The Bible says, "In him we live and move and have our being" (Acts 17:28). The Bible also says that those who worship must "worship in the Spirit and in truth" (John 4:24). If that is the case, then we must come to God in our true conditions. Like Jacob, we can't continue to run from who we are or who we are destined to be.

Jacob was exhausted from trying to be something other than what he was. That's the lesson. His wrestling reveals that no matter what we do in our own efforts, we cannot change ourselves. And, in truth, this is the entirety of the gospel. Jacob's story hints at the gospel but it became fully actualized through Jesus Christ in the New Testament. We are helpless on our own to redeem ourselves. In 2 Corinthians 5:17, we read, "Therefore if any man be in Christ, he is a new creature" (KJV). A new creature receives a new name. The moment Jacob resigned to be his honest, authentic, broken self, God said, "Your name will no longer be Jacob, but Israel, for you have contended with God and with man, and have prevailed."

When Jacob told the truth, he unlocked the blessing. The lesson for all of us is that God is looking for truth. He can change our nature, but we have to be honest about our nature. We have to be honest with where we are. That's the wrestling. The wrestling is the unveiling of our truth. The wrestling is the unveiling of the uncomfortable thing that we wish to be hidden or remain anonymous. We can no longer walk around hoping that no one sees the bleeding from behind our garments, the massive wound that never heals. In that singular moment when God changed his name, Jacob—now Israel—went from a life of running to a life of relevance. He moved from a life of pain and being pursued to a life of patriarchal prominence, from a life of ignominious brokenness to a limitless eternity. His seed will go on forever and ever. His offspring will be known for all eternity. All because he told the truth, and the truth wasn't savory.

The truth wasn't flowery. It wasn't romantic. It was not fragrant. In fact, it was a sweaty, pungent, unattractive thing. Jacob essentially told God, "I am every sneaky, broken thing I've ever done, and I am here in the middle of the desert because all I know how to do is run." And God took his brokenness and made him whole. So many people have orchestrated their lives to avoid the conflict of facing their true selves in an effort to trick people into thinking that they're something they're actually not. What an exhausting enterprise it must be to live a life hoping to please people with a truth that is not yours. Here's a secret: God is actually looking for the authentic you, not the projected you. The you He created is the you He can redeem. But He will not redeem what is projected as perfection and what is assumed as autonomous.

Where is the place, the one thing, that's separating you from victory? It's not your strength. It's not your intellect. It's not your ability. God is looking for truth, and he's going to ask you a question, and if you answer the question correctly, everything else in your life will come to order. Everything else in your life will unfold. Everything else in your life will make sense. What gives God glory is when broken

people tell the truth and then allow God to give them a
new identity. A new perspective. This allows our lives to be
a testimony and beacon of hope for those who say there's
no way an eternal God could love them. Victory for Jacob
came when he looked within and was able to tell the truth
about his condition. When he did, God immediately gave
him a new name. He didn't have to run anymore, because
when God gives you a name, everything changes.

Hold On

> Then the man said, "Your name will no longer be
> Jacob, but Israel, because you have struggled with
> God and with humans and have overcome." (Genesis
> 3:28)

What's also intense is that, essentially, the angel was
saying, "You won!" But Jacob won by losing. He didn't
win the wrestling match, but God declared him the victor.
So the victory wasn't in the actual winning, the victory
was in holding on. That is what I hoped I've conveyed
in this book. Winning is about holding on. Those old
church hymns got it right. We must hold on to God's
unchanging hand. We must hold on to His promise. We
must hold on to His word when it doesn't make sense,
when no one else can see, and when we can't even see the
outcome ourselves.

When you've had an encounter with God like Jacob's, your life is never the same. No one has to force you to worship. No one forces you to give. Nothing is forced when you've seen God face-to-face, when you've touched the divine presence of the living God.

CHAPTER TEN

When the Past Comes Knocking

We never get away. We can never escape, no matter how long we run, no matter how far we travel. And it's not the vehicle by which we run that matters. Doesn't matter if we run by train, plane, or automobile, the engine that drives the dysfunction in our lives is too often the face that stares back at us in the mirror. And so when the past comes knocking, when everything we've tried to avoid comes back to greet us and we're sitting in a room with all our regrets and all our unattended issues waiting for us to deal with them one by one, this is a sure sign that confrontation is inevitable. If we're ever going to be who God intended for us to be, we need to deal with the fact that our Esau is coming! The thing we thought we could avoid is coming. Whether publicly or privately, exposure *is* coming, because God doesn't let any of us get away.

One of the traits that God develops in leaders is this uncomfortable necessity of facing the hardest places unflinchingly. God is a master of putting people in positions where they have to deal with the things they would instinctively run from. Jacob's life was a case study in track and field. He would run from trouble. He would run from conflict. He was not a fighter. He ran. And I get it because I, too, have never been one for conflict. I learned early on that I'm a diplomat, not a warrior, and I tried to make peace because I wasn't going to fight. Jacob wasn't going to fight. Jacob was a used-car salesman. He talked his way out of things. He figured ways to get over. In chapter 33 of Genesis, we see what running can do for you. You become skittish. You become afraid. You assume everybody's coming after you because of the things that you've done, and in Genesis 33, we see Esau coming after Jacob with four hundred men.

Now, up to this point, everything in the relationship between Jacob and Esau had been fractured, severed, and for all Jacob knew, when Esau caught up to him he was going to kill him. Imagine living with the fear of looking over your shoulder because you did somebody wrong. Before we shake our collective heads, let us remember the moments where we've not done everything correctly in a relationship, the people we weren't totally forthcoming with, or moments where we made bad decisions and left ourselves open to ridicule, vulnerability, and the fear of being potentially exposed or shamed for the things we've done. Jacob was in a very similar position. It happened at the worst possible time, because for all of Jacob's life he had been able to run. That was his M.O. He ran emotionally. He ran physically. He ran relationally. He only dealt with things that pleased him.

We all have these things that we run from and run to. The ability to have a life of great value and meaning, a fruit-bearing, well-lived life, is contingent upon the disciplines you run from and toward. Some of us run from correction. We run from adjustment. We run from accountability. Ultimately our lives bear the fruit of an uncorrected, unadjusted, unaccountable life. Then there are others of us who run toward correction. We run to accountability. We run to community, and our lives bear the fruit of a well-adjusted and accountable life.

Your life will bear the fruit of what you run to. Jacob was in no shape to run. In Genesis 33, he is fresh off a cosmic wrestling match between heaven and earth, between the living God and a running man. What a vulnerable place to be, when we can't run anymore. Even if we wanted to, we don't have the ability to, because God has touched us. You will know that God wants to mature you and graduate you to a place of substantive relevance when he shrinks the thing that you used to use as a mechanism to run from responsibility, to run from what could and should mature you. Jacob couldn't run. God shrunk his hip. But what

Jacob didn't understand was that God didn't just touch his hip. God had changed his heart.

Esau had carried anger and bitterness for years. We don't know his process, but when the Bible says that Jacob saw Esau coming with four hundred men and he divided his estate up and placed his children, wives, and property in front and some in back, it was likely because Jacob wasn't sure what Esau was going to do. Jacob surrounded himself with what he thought would give him a buffer. It's almost like he was offering Esau these things. "See, look. Don't kill me. I got kids. Look, I got this stuff." Ordinarily, though, when someone is coming after you, it doesn't matter what you offer him. If you've wronged him and he's determined, there's nothing you can do.

When the past comes knocking, you can often end up discounting the power of God because of a tough circumstance or an individual's perceived authority. But remember, God didn't just touch Jacob's hip, he touched his heart. And because he had touched his heart, he changed his name. But God didn't just change Jacob's name. He changed Jacob's nature. He gave his new nature a new name and therefore a new identity. When Esau shows up, instead of killing Jacob, he embraces Israel. Even though Esau and Jacob were blood-related, when God touched Jacob's hip, he didn't just change his physical posture, God changed him on a cellular level. Therefore, Esau could not deal with Israel the same way he would have dealt with Jacob.

You Are Different and the Same

When Esau saw who he thought was Jacob, he embraced the very person he was determined to kill, because he wasn't the same as Esau remembered. Something in Israel's eyes let Esau know, "This is not the same brother who stole my birthright. This is not the same person." Instead of attacking him, Esau embraced him. Sometimes God will allow moments from your past to come into your present, to show you that he can redeem your mistakes. I'm sure Jacob was shocked. He likely didn't understand why his brother was holding him instead of beating him. He probably hadn't realized that the image Esau was privy to was a man God had just touched. For many people, the power of transformation is the calling card of a living God. Many people need to see a full picture of what we used to be versus who we are once the Lord gets His hands on us. Sometimes we need to see it too.

None of us are perfect, and before we can embrace our royal nature, we must remember that it wasn't something that we earned. God just put His hand on us. When the past comes knocking, instead of bowing to it, we need to bow to the God who is in control of it. It's a beautiful thing that the Bible says, "As far as the east is from the west, he casts our sins and remembers them no more" (see Ps. 103:12), and so, when the past comes knocking, we must determine that we can answer and answer that door with a smile and say, "Yes, I remember you. I remember who I was when I did these things, but I'm not that man now. I'm not that woman now. I'm not that person now, and I don't have to be held hostage to the worst version of myself."

Too many in our society, and even in our faith traditions, prize shame over mercy, redemption, and reconciliation. Yet it is the relentless love of God that ran after us when we weren't even looking for Him. That gives us value. The enemy thrives on the past because it's all he has. God doesn't dwell in the past. God dwells in perpetual *nowness*. He exists in this moment as he existed sixteen trillion years ago and sixteen trillion years before that. The reason why the past doesn't matter is because when we submit our life to Christ and we have committed to the blood of Jesus, the past has no authority to dictate or determine the trajectory of our future. Yes, it is critical to learn the lessons of the past so that you don't make the same mistakes going forward. But you can be sure that when the past comes knocking, it's the enemy's final attempt to get you to see yourself as you were, not as you are or as you shall be. Many people are saddled with years of stagnation due to the regret of bad decisions, and they talk themselves out of a future of love and wholeness and beauty because the past whispers "Unworthy." The devil uses unworthiness and shame and guilt to attempt to keep us from seeing, embracing, and acknowledging the finished work of Jesus.

There's always an Esau somewhere. Esau is not always a person. Esau could be a memory. Esau could be a habit.

Esau could be an old addiction. Esau could be an old flame. Esau could be someone we've done wrong in our past or something we've done wrong. And because most people have a seed of good, they don't want to go around being known for what they did wrong. The devil knows that, and he plays on that emotion—the need to be validated, the need to be seen as good—but the truth is, Jacob wasn't good and he didn't have the tools to be good. Many of us who have made bad decisions did not make them with all the information. Give yourself the same grace that the Lord gives us. The power of God is that He saw who we would be in totality and still chose to bless us, to love us, to use us.

Esau is representative of everything we've ever been afraid of, everything we've ever done wrong, everything we think is coming back to haunt us when we get into our blessed place. Esau is representative of a mindset that says, "I can't enjoy too much because what if somebody finds out that I wasn't always this person?" The truth is, we were never always one thing. Everyone has a story. Everyone has a testimony. Everyone has places where they wished they could change and have made better decisions. Only Jesus Christ Himself had no regrets, and so when your past comes knocking, answer the door. Give it a smile and say, "I'm glad to see you. I learned the lesson, but you're not welcome in this new place. I was Jacob, but I'm Israel now."

Let me encourage you with this: each human being has a calling from God. Not everyone will walk it out, because we have free will. But for those who submit their lives to the

Lord, you have a calling and a purpose to fulfill. Don't disqualify yourself simply because you've made bad decisions. God factored in your humanity when He called you. Not one thing you or I have done has caught God off guard. He is intimately aware of the things we have done that are wrong and still chose to write a chapter in the book where we are victorious.

Stop trying to rewrite what God has already written. Our stories are the finished work that the world is reading. Stop trying to give the devil a pen. The devil doesn't have a say unless you give him one. The Bible says Jesus is the author and finisher of our faith, so the devil can only read your story. Your story is finished and there's no shame attached to it. There is no guilt or condemnation attached, because Scripture says, "There is therefore now no condemnation to them which are in Christ Jesus, who walk not after the flesh, but after the Spirit" (Rom. 8:1 KJV).

Live your life. Grow in grace. Don't let your past determine your present or your future. The shame of bad decisions gives way to the refreshing forgiveness found in the blood, and when the Esaus come, acknowledge them. When necessary, apologize. Do your best to make amends. If that's not enough, you move on and let God handle it. Esau's not a place to dwell. It's a lesson to learn.

So let the past knock, and as soon as you let it go, the future is right behind it. Let your future in. Let your destiny in. Let your purpose in. Let your calling in, and watch that take you to places you could never get to on your own.

This is the power of learning the lessons from your past, never repeating the mistakes through the power of the Holy Spirit, but then embracing this new creation in Christ and moving forward. You should probably put this book down, because I think you got a knock at the door. Your future is calling. You should answer it.

CHAPTER ELEVEN

Allow Me to Reintroduce Myself

I was on a plane one day when I heard someone say, "You're John Gray. And I am number eight." When I turned, it was an African American woman who, I later learned, was to have a tremendously successful career in a Fortune 500 company. She said, "I was just introduced to you and your book through one of my friends. At this moment in my career, I'm realizing that I am a number eight because God is doing things in my life that have never been done." She continued to share with me how good God had been to her and what He'd been doing. It was truly a pleasure to speak with her and hear her story. But what caught me by surprise, what stuck with me, wasn't all the things she told me. It was her first words: "I was just introduced to you." She had never met me, but she had been introduced to me. I had been introduced based on someone else's recommendation. She "knew" me based on someone else's lens and perspective.

Even more interesting was the fact that she identified me based on the way she was introduced to me. She'd listened to my sermons and read my previous book, so she knew me as a pastor. That's not the only thing I am, but it's how she knew me. So when we met on that plane to Australia, in many ways I had to reintroduce myself. We had additional conversations, and in those conversations more information was exchanged. She got to know a little bit more about me than she previously knew, and while she might have begun the trip identifying me as one thing, by the time we disembarked, she had got to know me as someone else totally. It's one thing to know of a person, it's another to know a person.

The God Who Redefines

Jacob left his wrestling match in the dust of the desert, different and the same. The man who emerged was the man who had always been there, the one he always wanted to be. And that is the power of winning from within. When we dig deep and find the will to persevere and face the things we'd rather not, people might remember what we used to do. But by the power of God, they will also be introduced to who we actually are. The reintroduction of Jacob as *Israel* is the most profound transformation in all of Scripture prior to the Mount of Transfiguration.

The grace and power of God is truly found in the power of redefinition, repurposing, and restoring. God specializes in reintroducing His children. He reclaims us off the trash heap of stupid decisions and relationships that bore no fruit; of endless job searches and meandering through life trying to grope about in the darkness; of trying to figure it out. And then one night—or over many years—we wrestle with the deep things and He gives us the key to who we actually are. The power of reintroduction is the power of becoming.

One of the most significant challenges for any person walking with a "new name" is the battle of worthiness. People who have been called by God, even me, can find themselves feeling like they don't deserve it. We ask, Does this gift, this calling, really belong to me? Is this really my life? It's easy to look around and see the opportunities that God has given you and feel deeply unworthy.

But what I've come to realize, and I think what Jacob came to realize, is that everything he had was God's idea, not his. God is the one in control. He is the one who worked everything out for our good. Reintroduction was not just about Jacob being reintroduced to the world; it was also about God reintroducing Himself to Israel.

So one of the things that is critical and essential is to identify who you are and to be clear about how people once knew you. For Jacob, he was known as the trickster. That was clear. We've talked about his name and all that it meant and all that was attached to it. But God in His providence and sovereignty decided that Jacob, the trickster, was going to become Israel, a prince with God and a man who would prevail. We see God take a man who was known for one thing, touch him, and reintroduce him as someone entirely different.

What's significant about the touch of God on anybody's life is that whoever you were before God touches you, that person cannot remain. When God puts his hand on you, you're never the same. When He decides to change your name, the identity you were once known for is no longer valid or valuable.

Jacob didn't just win at Peniel, the name he gave to the place where he wrestled with God, the place where God touched him and gave him his limp. He prevailed. And that prevailing was not about victory as much as it was about engagement. God wants us to engage the thing that we are ashamed of, the things that cause us the most discomfort, so he can redefine our narrative and give new meaning to our pain.

The Day before the Miracle

When we examine the text outlining Jacob's wrestling match with God, it's easy to focus on the miracle. The name change. The entrance into destiny. But I think it's also important to pay attention to what happened the day before the miracle. For Jacob, he'd surrendered. He was tired of running and was prepared to face his past. I think that surrendered place is an important part of this journey.

See, everybody thinks they are ready for the miracle, but it's what you do on the day before that positions you to receive what's coming the next day. Some days seem to have an endless supply of trouble and worry. So much so, it can leave you questioning your purpose in God's creation. You might even wonder if you'll ever reach your intended destination. You might ask, "Will I ever win?"

Well, what are you willing to lose? Are you willing to surrender it all like Jacob? That's the posture you need to be prepared for the miracle. Are you ready to rest and simply trust in God? Are you willing to wrestle God and not let go until He blesses you? That's the posture you need to be prepared for the miracle.

I firmly believe we should all look at what's coming into our lives from the perspective of a checkers board. Everyone knows that when you play checkers, your checker pieces are on one side and your opponent's are on the other. If you make enough of the right moves, you get to the other side of the board and your opponent has to "king" you (return one of the pieces they stole from you as a crown of sorts). When one gets a king, they can make moves that the other player cannot make. And so it goes with our lives on this journey to winning God's way. You're waiting on a miracle and God is waiting on you to make a move. And—get this—sometimes you'll make a move and realize that you've got some authority over things that you thought should have been miracles. Some of us are asking for things that don't require miracles. Sometimes our request for a miracle is actually a veiled opportunity to develop discipline.

The God of the House

In this book, I've covered the two major encounters Jacob had with God as he was navigating his process. Jacob wrestled with God and named the place where he wrestled Peniel (God's Face). Jacob's first encounter with God was when he had a dream and saw angels ascending and descending a ladder. When that encounter was done, he named the place Bethel, or House of God. But there is one more event I think is significant. It occurs after Jacob received his new name and after he reconciled with his past (Esau).

> Esau said, "Oh, brother. I have plenty of everything—keep what is yours for yourself." Jacob said, "Please. If you can find it in your heart to welcome me, accept these gifts. When I saw your face, it was as the face of God smiling on me. Accept the gifts I have brought for you. God has been good to me and I have more than enough." Jacob urged the gifts on him and Esau accepted.
>
> Then Esau said, "Let's start out on our way; I'll take the lead."

But Jacob said, "My master can see that the children are frail. And the flocks and herds are nursing, making for slow going. If I push them too hard, even for a day, I'd lose them all. So, master, you go on ahead of your servant, while I take it easy at the pace of my flocks and children. I'll catch up with you in Seir."

Esau said, "Let me at least lend you some of my men."

"There's no need," said Jacob. "Your generous welcome is all I need or want."

So Esau set out that day and made his way back to Seir.

And Jacob left for Succoth. He built a shelter for himself and sheds for his livestock. That's how the place came to be called Succoth (Sheds).

And that's how it happened that Jacob arrived all in one piece in Shechem in the land of Canaan—all the way from Paddan Aram. He camped near the city. He bought the land where he pitched his tent from the sons of Hamor, the father of Shechem. He paid a hundred silver coins for it. Then he built an altar there and named it El-Elohe-Israel (Mighty Is the God of Israel). (Genesis 33:9–20 MSG)

So why was there a difference between the name Jacob gave the place where God showed him the ladder and the name he gives the place where he eventually pitches his tent? What's the difference between Bethel (House of God) and El-Elohe-Israel (Mighty is the God of Israel)? The difference is as simple as a name change. It was *Jacob* who called the place of the first encounter the house of God. And it was *Israel* who called the place of reconciliation Mighty is the God of Israel. Because in the wrestling—in the reintroduction—Jacob/Israel got a revelation that he wasn't just in the house of God; he had encountered the God of the house.

When Your Past Sees You Anew

As I noted earlier, at the point of reconciliation, Esau came running up toward Jacob and his camp with four hundred men. He arrived to find Jacob bowed low (see Gen. 33:1–4). In many ways, this was a sign of humility and repentance. It was Jacob's way of saying, "I'm humbling myself. Please don't kill me." But Esau doesn't kill him. Why? This is the same man who stole his birthright. Or is it? Esau doesn't kill him because he no longer saw Jacob. He saw Israel. He saw something different in his brother even if he couldn't readily identify it. This is the essence of what is now called restorative justice. Reconciliation is hard. It's a huge gamble. However, at the core of godly restoration is the ability to see our brother or sister the way that God sees them.

Esau saw the touch of God on Jacob's life. He saw the evidence of that touch in the limp. I must reiterate that in order for any man or woman of God to truly be seen anew after a touch of God, they must identify their limp. They must be willing to allow their limitations to be seen.

God reintroduced Jacob to the world as Israel, and the evidence of the journey was clear. The change was clear. The limp pointed to his change of character and his shift in vision. Israel had wisdom and discernment in areas that Jacob did not. Jacob was shortsighted. Jacob was everything we know him to be. He was not a visionary. He lived for the moment and made impulsive decisions. But God knew that Israel was inside him. And it was Israel who would fulfill the promises and plans He had for the world. Jacob didn't need sons. Israel did. They are known as the children of Israel, not the children of Jacob. As his seed, his children and his children's children received the benefit of his name change.

God has the ability to reintroduce us. Our worst moments and mistakes, our bad habits and patterns, the proclivities that we are known for, they can all be changed if we will allow God to touch us. We must be willing to allow God to reach into that place that needs to be submitted. For Jacob, it was his hip, because he was always running. For others, it's a heart, because sometimes our hearts are too hard. For others, it's our mind, because we have idolized our intellect. Still for others, it's our tongue, because we talk too much. Sometimes it's our flesh, because we do things that are outside of God's will. Whatever it is, we need to identify the place and submit it to God so He can touch it. Let Him shrink it so we can be seen differently. So we can see ourselves differently.

A New Mantle

Let's not get hung up on semantics. I don't want everyone running to the social security office, telling the people that God has changed their name. It's not just about consonants and vowels. What happened to Jacob is a metaphor for what God wants to do in our lives. It's about an identity shift that God confers. It's about the different mantle that comes with that new identity. When God changes us, he often changes our mantle. He changes the manifestation of our purpose. And that new mantle, the new manifestation, comes with increased responsibility. Don't worry though. That increase in responsibility comes with supernatural enablement, an innate knowing. You will surprise yourself. God will speak to you. When God changes your "name," he changes your position. And with that, He elevates and unlocks your mind.

And remember, it's not just about us being reintroduced to people. It's also—maybe even more so—God reintroducing Himself to us in new and fresh ways, ways that impact not just ourselves but everyone connected to us. At the end of his life, the man formerly known as Jacob was able to declare identity over each one of his sons. He was able to prophesize who they would be and what their impact would be (see Gen. 49). Jacob would not have been able to do that, but Israel absolutely could. Israel had the mantle.

No Going Back

Israel couldn't go back. He could no longer be Jacob. He had a word from God, and that was the end of who he once was. This goes for us too. We can't go back to who we were before. The journey to winning God's way is about being willing to even lose who you always believed yourself to be. And maybe even the people who bought into that person. Don't go back. You are different now. I am different now.

I've noted this throughout the book, but I want to emphasize it here: the danger inherent in trusting God for your future is losing the comfort of the familiar. We must become uncomfortable with comfort. That's the only way we are going to truly live.

Before you die, I need you to live. Too many people exist but do not live. They exist to pay bills, to make ends meet, to keep the status quo. They play it safe. They do nice things, but they're afraid to go after great things because greatness requires stretching. It requires faith, moving, the shedding of the familiar. It means letting go of what was yours and releasing it to someone else. So many people are afraid to become what God wants them to become because they're so committed to what they used to be. We are committed to our comfort.

So many of us like to know where everything is in our lives. We know how much is in our savings account down to the dime. We say, "I'm going to check my 401(k), you know, I've got benefits." And those things by themselves aren't bad at all. But as God is shifting us and pointing us toward our purpose, there *will* be times when we won't know everything. And that's okay. That's not the time to worry. In fact, God is like, "You're worrying about stuff that's not even going to last." We must, as the old church hymn says, "build our hopes on things eternal." We have to keep an eye on eternity while still being honorable with the things that we have to do on the earth.

Is there anything worse than living without a dream? It motivates you to stick it out while you're sitting in traffic. It motivates you while you're at a job that may not be completely fulfilling but is necessary so that you can make a living and pay bills while your dream is yet to manifest. But it isn't just about dreams—it's about ladders. Like Jacob all those years ago, I believe that God's getting ready to extend a ladder. He's getting ready to make a way out of no way, and you'll be climbing where angels climb.

Some of us have been sitting at a particular level for too long. God needs us to get a different vision from a different vantage point. From where we are, things look big, but when we get higher, that stuff that was big gets small real fast. Yes, we must be willing to do whatever it takes to make the dream come to pass. But we also need a ladder: the supernatural enabling power of the Holy Ghost. The work, the skill, the gift, the grind—none of this is enough. There are lots of people who work and have skill and gifts and they grind, but they are spinning their wheels because they have no anointing, no Holy Ghost, and no favor of God.

So when you get a word from God on top of your work, stand full and strong in that. Don't be tempted to go back to your own self, your old name. Ephesians 2:8–10 says, "For by grace you have been saved through faith, and this not from yourselves; it is the gift of God, not a result of works, so that no one may boast. For we are His workmanship, created in Christ Jesus for good works, which God prepared beforehand that we should walk in them" (ESV). God is looking for somebody who, if there is one second left on the clock and the ball is in their hands, wouldn't pass it to anybody else. You've gone through enough to know that the distance between you and that basket is not going to stop you from shooting this shot. It may not be straight, but it's going in some way or another. You want to win God's way, so you are not going to let opposition stop you. Now that you have reintroduced yourself, you are going to shoot your shot.

The Model, the Mirror, and the Moment

Now that we, like Jacob, have this word from God, there will absolutely be people who will try to close in on us. There will be situations that will try to close in on us.

Depression, religion, and other people's small expectations of us might try to suffocate us. The truth is, our freedom is awfully attractive to those in bondage. Don't worry about this though.

When you reintroduced yourself, when you shot the shot, you made a prophetic declaration that every enemy that's tried to hold you hostage has been utterly destroyed. Circumstances told you to give up, but you were like, "I ain't going nowhere. This is mine." Good for you! Your life told you to give up and you said, "I ain't going nowhere!" Praise God!

As you are coming to understand who God has declared you to be, you'll want to get serious about those dreams that were revealed. There are three things you need to identify and address: the models, the mirror, and the moment. I've talked about some of these throughout the book, but as I'm closing, I want to make sure that I leave you with something that will push you on toward your goal.

What is the model? The models are the forces that shape you. Models are represented by the people who raised you, the friends you came up around. Remember our discussion about the role of our history and family dynamics? Your models came from that history. Models are always those forces outside of your control that informed you.

You didn't determine where you were born or what you looked like. You didn't determine the predispositions in your DNA. You didn't determine the people who were addicted before you got here. You weren't able to fight against the people who abused you, who snatched your innocence. These were all things that, for good or bad, molded you. But even though they were outside of your control, they were not outside of God's control. And even if they happened and it was horrible, God allowed it. He didn't want it to happen but he knew because of free will people would do what they did. And despite their free will, God's will for your life will still be accomplished.

Note: I know I told you not to go back. That still holds. We aren't going back to those places. We aren't revisiting who we were prior to God speaking to our hearts. We are *looking* back—in gratitude. Thank God that what was supposed to kill you didn't do anything but *make* you.

Besides the model, there is the mirror. The mirror is the place where you begin to become aware of who you are, but more importantly, who you can become. As I noted earlier, sometimes the people around us, the ones closest to us, can serve as a mirror. They can help us see ourselves because that's what mirrors do—they reflect our true selves back to us. The selves that sit outside of the models that formed us. I'm more than where I was raised. I'm more than the abandoned son of a father who couldn't see me. I'm more than the four-year-old boy who was sexually abused by two teenagers on my front lawn. I'm more than the dude that used to get talked about every day on the school bus going to Withrow High School. I'm more than the guy that couldn't get the phone numbers of the girls I liked in high school. I'm more than the shame and the guilt of emerging manhood and the hormones and all of the things that come with being a teenager. I'm more than the stuff the devil tried to put on me. I've got a destiny that's bigger than this, and so do you. When you begin to realize that the things that made you can't stop you, God shifts you from model to mirror, where you will see what God intended through those lessons. You become aware of what you could become. It's where you face the areas of your life that aren't glamorous, but you still remain faithful. Have you ever remained faithful even though it was hard?

The mirror is where you stop lying to yourself. There is no filter and the reflection doesn't talk back. All it does is show you you—if you're willing to see. I believe God is saying to all of us, "I want to grow you up. I want to take you someplace else, but before I do I need to show you *you*. Take the spiritual makeup off. Take off all that extra stuff so that I can show you that you're beautiful without all of that."

Finally, there is the moment. Jacob had his after wrestling with the angel. But his was not an isolated case in Scripture. Let me move from Jacob to Elisha really quickly, to make this point:

Elijah went and found Elisha son of Shaphat plowing a field. There were twelve teams of oxen in the field, and Elisha was plowing with the twelfth team. Elijah went over to him and threw his cloak across his shoulders and then walked away. Elisha left the oxen standing there, ran after Elijah, and said to him,

"First let me go and kiss my father and mother good-bye, and then I will go with you!"

Elijah replied, "Go on back, but think about what I have done to you." So Elisha returned to his oxen and slaughtered them. He used the wood from the plow to build a fire to roast their flesh. He passed around the meat to the townspeople, and they all ate. Then he went with Elijah as his assistant. (1 Kings 19:19–21 NLT)

This was the moment for Elisha. He was behind the yoke of oxen with dirt and feces kicking up into his face. But he had remained faithful to stay in the field, because that was the call on his life. And while he was faithful in the mess, here comes the prophet, and the prophet throws his mantle onto Elisha and, in so many words, says, "It's time." Now, what do you do once you're in the moment and you get the double portion?

You don't die without giving it all away.

Elisha died, and they buried him. And the bands of the Moabites invaded at the coming in of the year. And it came to pass, as they were burying a man, that, behold, they spied a band of men; and they cast the man into the sepulcher of Elisha: and when the man was let down, and touched the bones of Elisha, he revived, and stood on his feet. (2 Kings 13:20–21 KJV)

Whoa! That's a powerful anointing. The Scriptures say that the *moment* the dead man touched Elisha's bones, he got up. Now sure, that's a miracle, but I've always been concerned, because after everything Elisha had to go through to get that anointing, why didn't he think enough of it to give it to anybody else? Great, this man got up, but does anybody know the man's name? The Bible essentially says he was just a *guy*. Which brings me to my point: at the moment of transfer, when God pours His anointing out on your life and reveals His plan for you, and after all that you've gone through to get to that point, make a commitment to die empty.

Don't die anointed. Die dry. Die exhausted. Leave nothing in the grave. When the time comes for you to transition, be able to say without any doubt that everything you were created to do, you did it. I don't want to die and get to heaven and God is like, "What are you doing here?"

"I'm supposed to be here. I accepted Jesus."

"Yeah, but you got here early."

"What do you mean?"

"Because you didn't take care of your body."

Ouch.

Our temples house the purpose of God. We must be good stewards of the purpose God has placed down in us. We all have a personal responsibility to help God get the maximum glory out of our lives. When you were being healed from the cancer that was supposed to take your life, I guarantee you weren't at the fast-food restaurants every day eating whatever you wanted. You probably took care of yourself, ate good things, got plenty of rest. There are certain things that you and I can do to extend and expand our life, to make sure that we are physically able to do what we were created to do.

That was for me, but maybe it was for you too.

Nevertheless, assessing your moment is really about doing everything you can to die dry. Don't take one idea to your grave with you. Try all the witty inventions God has given you. Do them all. Are you trying to be a bestselling author? Great. You want to write a movie? Do that. You praise dance? Get it. People of God, don't miss the moment. You may have a lot of days, but you won't get a lot of moments. When the moment comes, you better take it. When God opens that door, you better go. When he opens that window, you better shoot your shot.

How Though?

You want to win. You have your word. You've faced your past. God has "changed your name" and reintroduced you to the world. You have identified your models, assessed your mirrors, and are standing in your moment. What do you do?

First, ask yourself: What's the dream? Be clear about what God has shown you. What's that thing God put in your heart that you were created to do? Next: Who's your team? Who's close enough to help you build? This is where your discernment must kick in. Know who God has called you to, and who He's called to you, in this season. Finally, ask yourself, What's my seed? Don't think you're going to get something great without sowing something. What are you willing to sow and seed in order to get the breakthrough? For some, that will require substance. Some will need to sow into their family. Others will need to get things right with their brother or their sister or their mom or their dad. Whatever it is, you need that seed in the ground.

Identity = Time with the Savior

It is our time of engagement and encounter with Jesus that gives us the ability to grab our new identity. That's where our peace is found. Our identities are not tied up in our behavior. My identity is not tied up in what other people see in me or how they perceive me. My identity is tied up in Jesus Christ alone. The finished work of Jesus has given me access to the resources of heaven. So as God elevates us, he reintroduces us. People who knew us as one thing are shocked when they see the same body but not the same person. This is the power of an inside change that has an outward manifestation.

I'm seeing this reintroduction even in my own marriage. My wife pushed me into places of relevance and greatness despite my inability at times to face my responsibilities. She has loved me and pushed me and covered me. I'm grateful that she chose to stay with me while I learned. Yes, there were some moments there when the enemy attacked us—when I thought I would lose everything. But God was setting us up to win. My wife fought and prayed, and because she did, we are experiencing a harvest. She stayed through the warfare and now she's seeing the harvest; she's seeing the fruit.

The reintroduction is an inner work that has an outward fruit. Allow me to reintroduce myself:

My name is John. I've engaged with God and I've allowed Him into my uncomfortable places. I've allowed Him into my places of shame, doubt, and guilt. God is healing me daily and I'm looking forward to seeing the best version of myself as I grow in Him.

CHAPTER TWELVE

Winner Leaves All

If there are any words that an individual or people should especially consider, it's what someone says when they know they are dying. As her days were coming to a close, my maternal grandmother, Maine Davis, spoke with words that carried greater weight than anything else I'd heard. But her words worked in tandem with the life she lived. Yes, I have the memory of her words, but I also have the evidence of the life she lived as she said them. That gave her authority.

Even though brain cancer had taken her hair, it had not taken my grandmother's mind. I remember holding her hands and praying for her, when she said, "I feel the power of God in your hands, I feel the power of God in your hands." Until the end, my grandmother believed God for her healing, but she was never afraid of death, because she taught her children and her grandchildren that there was something greater once this life is over.

It wasn't the first time she'd spoken over my life. My grandmother prophesied over me many times, and all the things she prophesied are coming true. When someone with authority, who hears from God and can speak from the mind of God, says something, you can take it to the bank. Ask the sons of Jacob.

In Genesis 49, we find Jacob at the end of his life and prophesying destiny over his sons. In the first and second verses he says, "Gather around so I can tell you what will happen to you in days to come. Assemble and listen, sons of Jacob; listen to your father Israel." Then he proceeds to outline the destiny of each and every son. The death of Jacob was a sacred moment, but it's also an instructional one for those of us who are believers. We believe in a God who is the intelligent designer of the universe. We believe that we are not just a conglomeration of cells that haphazardly came together after a romantic encounter between a mother and father, but we are the intention of heaven for the attention of the earth, and we have a purpose bigger than our humanity can even declare. We know we are part of a story that started before us and will continue after us. And that should cause us to find great meaning in how Jacob approaches the end of his life. After all the life he had lived, all the experiences that he had, all that he had loved, and all that he had lost, after all the things that had gone wrong, and the many things that had gone right, he comes to the end and prophesies the continuation of what God had birthed in him.

My frame was not hidden from you when I was made in the secret place, when I was woven together in the depths of the earth. Your eyes saw my unformed body; all the days ordained for me were written in your book before one of them came to be. (Psalm 139:15–16)

To win from within is not about what one can accumulate throughout the course of a life. It's not about houses, land, accolades, notoriety. It's not about public celebration. It's about living a life of substance and value that leaves a legacy when your words have come to an end.

Anyone who wants to be successful must realize that success does not start with us, and no one gets to success without support. It is the responsibility of those who have been blessed with resources, platforms, or influence to not hoard them for ourselves, but to be good stewards, to see beyond our own days and into the legacy of the future. We are stewards of everything and owners of nothing. If we are wise with what God gives us, we can establish a legacy that will outlast us.

Declaring a Legacy

One of the reasons why I'm fascinated by this exchange between Jacob/Israel and his sons is because my own father never declared legacy over me. I longed for the validation of my earthly father. I longed for him to tell me what I was supposed to do. I needed him. I deeply desired his guidance in telling me how to live as a man, how to talk to girls, how to approach opportunities. But the truth is: that's not who he was, and that's not the information he had to give. I've learned that it is a challenge to give what you don't have. I found myself struggling many a night attempting to give to my wife what I never possessed in my soul. As I've shared, I longed to be the best husband and the best father, but I could not be what I'd never seen. At least not in my own strength.

As I consider what I desired from my own dad—that Jacob-esque outlining of my own destiny—I find myself in the same position. I hope to live a long life, but if I don't, I pray that what I have achieved, the way I've served, will outlast me.

I have two children at the writing of this book: my son, John Gray IV, and my daughter, Theory Aspyn-Sky. I've got one that carries my name and another that I will give away one day to someone with a different last name. With each of their births, I realized, maybe much like Jacob, that the microphones I hold around the world are no longer microphones. They are batons that will be passed on. What I do will echo for generations to come.

Principles for Life

I love Shakespeare. Larry Boyd was my drama teacher at Withrow High School in Cincinnati, an urban high school, which I suppose is a nice way of saying that we didn't have the resources and comforts of some of our suburban neighbors. But we did have a Shakespeare competition that was part of a citywide competition. I entered and ended up winning at my school, and I was sent to compete against other students in the city.

I will never forget a key part of my Shakespearean monologue. It was from *Julius Caesar*, and I believe it stuck with me because it's the truth about the human condition.

Friends, Romans, countrymen, lend me your ears;
I come to bury Caesar, not to praise him.
The evil that men do lives after them;
The good is oft interred with their bones.

How true it is of humankind that no matter how much good you do, it can be very easily forgotten, because the nature of the human condition is to remember every wrong thing you've ever done.

In Genesis 49, we see Jacob prophesying and declaring who his sons will be. To the letter, each one of his sons manifested what he said. Under divine revelation, he made these declarations, and this is where I believe we should model Jacob. Being victorious in life is about declaring and prophesying over the generation coming behind you. It's about speaking to them, resourcing them, offering direction, clarity, and the vision they need so that they can be more, go further, and fly higher.

That's not just a spiritual principle. That's a principle for any good business or relationship. The concept of legacy must be a part of the equation, if you are going to be known beyond your lifespan. Jacob prophesied, and every single thing he prophesied came to pass. So many of our children are longing for identity, and I believe it is a profound right of a parent or authority figure to speak destiny over the children.

I don't believe that life just happens. We have a mandate from God to declare destiny over our seed. We must declare destiny not just over the children we may have birthed naturally, but over all children who are broken, vulnerable, marginalized, and bullied. It is necessary that we are compassionate toward those who don't have advocates. Those of us who have been gifted with resources or influence need to use our gifts, ability, and platforms to fight for those who cannot fight for themselves and to shield the vulnerable ones from this oppressive season in the earth where so much vitriol and negativity is spoken and spewed.

What It Really Means to Win

Normally in big prizefights or "game seven" moments, it's winner take all. As I noted, Jacob's sons became every single thing he said they would become. This reveals to us that, in God's economy, it's not winner takes all, it's winner leaves all. Winners leave a legacy that lasts. If we live our lives right and walk our processes out, we won't take anything with us when we pass on. In fact, a true victorious life, a life that says, "I won," is a life that says, "I lost it all—but I lost it in the right places."

The truth is, we must be willing to lose our things to the people who need them the most. Jacob left it all. He took nothing with him. And so it goes with us. We must lose our wills to the will of the Father. We must lose our wealth to worthy causes and/or the leaving of an inheritance for our children's children. Winning is not about accumulating billions of dollars and having it all in our name when we die. Winning is building something that is so significant that it is multicultural, multigenerational, and multidenominational. The questions we ultimately must ask are: Is Jesus glorified? Did we draw people closer to Jesus? Do people want to serve the Lord because they encountered us?

If I live to be ninety, then I'm halfway home right now. What do I want people to know me for? There are many things I've done wrong, none of which I'm proud of. But there are a lot of things I've done right. One of the things I did right, I did early, when I gave my life to Jesus Christ. I've been walking with Him ever since, and although I've not done everything right, I've certainly held His hand even when I failed.

In essence, my faith has informed every decision I've ever made. When I think about what true victory looks like, it resembles a man who holds on to God's unchanging hand—no matter what. We all must identify something that is bigger than ourselves in order to truly win. We then must work toward that goal with legacy in mind.

When I think about my own legacy, I think about my family. Not just my children, but Aventer, my wife. She has put up with so much because of my insecurities. I almost lost my marriage because of them. What a tragedy it would have been to perpetuate the broken legacy of divorce and all of the accompanying effects to our children, including the respect of all the people who believe in us as leaders and who look to us as an example of perseverance. Aventer Gray has shown me, more than any other individual besides my mother, the unconditional love of Christ. She has been the greatest sermon I've ever seen. She's lived biblical truth and love in front of me, and has given me the ability to have a legacy. She birthed two children inside of eleven and a half months and has worked tirelessly toward every hope and dream I have spoken out of my mouth, even deferring her own dreams. When I think of my own "wins," I'm clear that I wouldn't be where I am without her. She's the best decision I ever made, because she's a decision I made in the spirit.

I say and pray for every person reading this book that when you choose a life partner, a husband or a wife, you choose based not simply on the cosmetics and the external aesthetic, but for legacy and long-term victory. Choose someone who will extend the ladder of your dream and push for your vision even when you are too weary to fight for it. That's what God gave me in Aventer. When I die, I plan to be buried next to her in a small nondescript burial plot in North Florida, in a little city called Campbellton. I will be buried in the red clay on the side of that beautiful little church off a country road not far from where my wife's parents grew up. Why there and not my hometown of Cincinnati? Why not Houston or Atlanta or New Jersey or any of the other cities I've lived in? The truth is, I just want to be where she is. I want to close my eyes knowing that I did right by her. I want to close my eyes knowing that I gave my children the best opportunity to fulfill their God-given calling.

For me, victory and being a winner in life is no longer about what I can achieve. I've traveled the whole world. I've preached everywhere. I've been afforded opportunities and privileges other people have never had. Now I just simply want to hear the Lord say, "Well done." Until then, I've got work to do. I've got children to raise. I've got a legacy to establish. I've got a wife to love. I've got curses to break. I've got bridges to build. I've got history to make. I've got leaders to develop and churches to strengthen.

I am committed to this work, and I am determined to do everything that God invested in me to do. What I cannot finish, my children will continue. That's the beauty of Jacob's prophetic declaration. He understood his place. This does not end with me. The kingdom will continue to press forward. The greatest place of victory is doing your part in pushing the kingdom forward. We are owners of nothing, but we are stewards of all things.

My prayer is that God will allow you and me to steward our respective places of position, prominence, and authority with the level of character and integrity that gives honor to the God who created us, and with a sobriety and prophetic understanding of the times we live in. We must work as hard as we can, serve as much as we can, and in the end prepare the way for those coming after us, so that one day we do indeed hear, "Well done."

The Grace Place

Jacob's journey is really a story of God's ever-present grace, a grace that pursues. My story is also one of relentless grace.

I suppose at the end of reading this book, many readers might be asking, "What about your marriage? Have things changed? Have *you* really changed?"

Here's what I know to be true: as much as I believe in process, I also believe that a person can be moving through life in a particular way, and in one moment everything turns. Whatever that person was doing, saying, or acting out before is over. The things that held him or her hostage simply fall away. In a single moment, they find themselves walking in a new level of freedom, clarity, and vision.

This is where I found myself when, on Sunday, June 3, 2018, I was installed as Senior Pastor of Relentless Church in Greenville, South Carolina.

In 1 Corinthians 15:9–11, the apostle Paul says, "For I

am the least of all the apostles. In fact, I'm not even worthy to be called an apostle after the way I persecuted God's church. But whatever I am now, it is all because God poured out his special favor on me—and not without results. For I have worked harder than any of the other apostles; yet it was not I but God who was working through me by his grace. So it makes no difference whether I preach or they preach, for we all preach the same message you have already believed" (NLT). I must echo the words of Paul when I think about the current state of my life. Whatever is good in my life, anything I've achieved, any measure of success or spiritual maturity, even this new role as a pastor, has only come by the grace of God.

What is this thing about God that He sees us in our brokenness and chooses to use us anyway? What is this thing about God that He loves us so much that he will not allow the brokenness of one moment to define the rest of our destiny? The day of installation, I finally recognized that my wife and I had been anointed as visionaries and pastors assigned to this particular region—in spite of any brokenness we had or still held. For the week leading up to that Sunday, I couldn't stop crying. I thought, *I can't believe God brought me to this place.* It blew my mind.

As I've mentioned earlier, from the youngest of ages, I never felt like I fit in. I was *that* kid, the one picked last for the teams on the playground. Being a single mom and having other familial obligations, my mom shopped for my clothes at yard sales and Goodwill. We struggled. And yet, there I was on Installation Sunday, with my measure of grace, pushing God's kingdom forward.

But my turning point wasn't about getting the pastorate. That was part of it: the first demonstration of God's grace in our new season. But it was what happened next that completed the shift.

Lots of people are great preachers and teachers. But if there is something in our character that is flawed, or something in our integrity that is slightly off, then it's incredibly easy to compromise on sin. I didn't want that. The gospel has been watered down and muddled over time because people don't want to offend others with the truth of the gospel. I wasn't interested in leading a country club where everyone came each week to feel good. God had called me to lead a church—people in need of a savior. We believe that Jesus died for all our sin.

Even mine.

I wasn't going to just preach at this church. I was going to participate as a member. The trouble with the Western church is that sometimes, many times, we elevate our leaders beyond ourselves. We expect them not to struggle. No, I'm very clear that I need the same blood the people in the pews need.

So I had to share my story. Our story.

I told this church that had just installed me as their pastor that I was a complete mess before I got there. I was a mess when God called me to them. I was battling with depression and other things that nobody knew about. And sadly, because I was gifted, pastors would count on me, call me to preach at their conferences, but only a few checked on me. (Gifted people often have their brokenness tolerated, and the subsequent foolish behavior that generally comes with it.) I wore the mask well. I wouldn't dare let them see a broken man, but secretly I wished they would have asked me, "How's your marriage? Are you taking care of your wife? Are you talking to anybody you don't need to be talking to?" But nobody knew to ask and I didn't tell them, because I was too afraid to tell the truth about the broken places that the enemy had held me hostage in since I was little.

I was preaching all around the world, and people had no clue that my family was falling apart. It was a vicious cycle. Yes, my gift was making room for me and bringing me before great people (see Prov. 18:16), but I knew that it was only my character that could keep me there. I didn't want cheap grace, where we can live how we want and do what we want and still be okay. God is not okay with sin. Sin cost Jesus His life. And if it cost Him His life, I knew I needed to serve Him with mine.

I believe that the office of a pastor should be one of utmost integrity, character, honor, and fidelity. And in light of the very real struggles I was having personally, as well as in my marriage, I found it strange that God would call me.

Yet God pursued me. And as much as He pursued me with His grace is as much as I remained persistent in doing His will. My brokenness didn't stop God from using me. I could still love God and struggle.

*   *   *

If I wanted to build artificial momentum upon becoming a pastor, I could have used my first sermon to declare the prosperity gospel—that everybody was getting a brand-new house and car. I could have talked about how everyone's bank account was going to overflow.

Instead, I chose to be transparent. I chose to lead from my scars. I chose to tell the truth. The challenge is, everybody can't handle the truth, because some people want your truth solely so they can talk about and expose you, to tear you down. But as a leader, I knew that it was important for this new congregation to know how far God had brought me. Grace lets you tell the truth because it's under the blood.

When you serve in ministry, people want your gift but not your truth. There were so many moments when Aventer and I had to stand before people with smiles on our faces when, meanwhile, at home, we were constantly in tears. I didn't know how to be a husband. I didn't know how to be a father. I was doing the best I could, yes, but I wrongly believed that as long as I preached and brought big numbers to churches, as long as I was able to provide, things would be okay.

People saw a pretty picture of a husband and wife. They didn't see a husband who was struggling and a wife who loved me back to life. Aventer fought, covered, prayed, interceded, and fought for me and my vision. Her nickname on social media is @grayceeme, and she has truly been a demonstration of grace for me.

When we first got married and had our first child, my constant travel and ministering elsewhere created both physical and emotional distance between us. That distance manifested into something bigger, and then all of the sudden, Satan was like, "She's your enemy." We were still in full-time ministry, and what was once just bad got even worse. The devil came after us with every gun blazing, and that kind of intense attack is what brought us to the moment that opens this book. It's what brought us to the question of whether or not we would continue being married. There was a point when my wife and I said, "Do we want to continue?"

But let me tell you what God did.

God extended to me a love so profound that it made no sense. I watched a woman I didn't even know how to love, how to cover, how to protect, how to honor, love me from my broken place. She knew the worst moments of my life and she said, "You get on my nerves, but I love you." Nobody else could reach the broken place but her.

So have *I* changed? I believe that my change began with telling the truth. By doing so, I put the devil under my feet.

How is my marriage? Well, we were once on the brink of divorce and now it's no longer an option. And not only are we never ever breaking up, nothing that the enemy tried to do is going to stand. It was nothing but God's grace that facilitated our breakthrough. And so it goes for everyone reading this.

No matter what you've been through in your relationships, you don't owe an explanation to your flesh, your family, or to any devil. If you're in a covenant, get it right with the person you're in covenant with. Let the devils do what they do—scatter like roaches. What I did in the past, and what you might have done, is not who we are. I am what I am by God's grace and the grace extended to me by my wife.

No matter where you are, when grace finds you, it immediately validates and heals you. The place of grace is the altar. We don't have anything of value to bring to Jesus except ourselves. And He will love you exactly where and how you are.

Sometimes the enemy will come after your marriage. For me, it was my own insecurities, my own fears and childhood traumas, that all collided in one place. And for a moment, I found myself listening to the lie of the enemy. But the devil is a liar. Divorce is a curse in my family and it could not stay. My wife and I are covenant bound.

Grace is not for the perfect; it's for the broken. Grace will pursue you. Ask Jacob. We don't have to stay stuck in our worst moments. And when we fall, grace catches us. Many times the phrase is used, "He fell from grace. She fell from grace." That's totally untrue. How do we "fall" from grace when grace is the floor? We never fall from grace, we fall *into* grace. Is it cheap? No. The cost of grace is death. But not ours. Jesus died so we might live. It's His grace that saves us. It heals us. The struggles of our past do not have to define our future.

A Prayer for You

Lord Jesus, for every person reading, I make a call for freedom. I lift up those of us who have desperately needed your grace. Some of us have been struggling with things since we were four years old. And, unfortunately, the church has never allowed us a space to be honest with what we're battling through. But today we pray for freedom. We hold tightly to your word that says "whom the Son sets free is free indeed!"

I also bind every devil that comes to attack readers at the point of their relationships. I declare that every spirit that comes to attack marriages is hereby arrested and expelled from our lives. I declare that the grace of God and the love of God that passes all understanding will begin to overtake us in every area of our lives. I bind petty devices that the enemy uses to bring about space and distance. I declare a resurgence and renaissance in the family.

Lord Jesus, please meet us at the point of our need. Fill us with deliverance and healing, miracles, signs, and wonders. Give us the strength to know that the thing that held us hostage had to let us go. And as each reader closes the pages of this book, allow each of them to embrace their freedom. Let them know that no one can hold anything over their head. We are not held hostage to our pasts. We are free from the sin and the shame.

The devil says, "Shame on you." Grace says, "Shame off you." So we love You, Father, and we give You honor.

In Jesus' name, amen.

Acknowledgments

This was the hardest thing I've ever done. Writing this book took longer than I could have ever anticipated—and for one simple reason: I can't write a book I haven't lived. It is my prayer that the words on these pages will impact your soul and ignite a ferocious desire to push through whatever obstacles you have that are stopping you from getting to the ultimate discovery: the power of an unlocked, unafraid, and unashamed YOU.

I want to thank my wife, Aventer, for being the test subject and closest observer to all that I've gone through and am becoming. I love you, and I'm thankful that God gave me a wife gracious enough to see what I was and where I was—yet stay anyway. Thank you, my love, for your supernatural patience and devotion. I love you forever.

To my children, John W. Gray IV and Theory Aspyn-Sky Gray. I love you with everything I have. I pray that the healed version of me is a better dad than the one you guys had for these first few years. You are a legacy only God could have created.

To my mom. Intercessor. Confidant. Cheerleader. Thank you for not letting me live in the place of shame and pain that bullying and childhood insecurities can produce. You spoke what could be and would become. And it's all coming to pass. I love you, Ma.

Many thanks to A. Y. and Bonnie Cotton, love you!

To my amazing co-laborer and resident button pusher, Tracey Lewis-Giggetts. Thank you for walking this path with me until this book was completed. You are a true literary genius, and I'm thankful for your wisdom and insight as we finished this monumental task.

To Jan, Shannon, and the entire Dupree-Miller team. Thank you for all you've done and continue to do. Let's keep going! To Monica Bacon. Thank you for always being there for me and for fighting for me in rooms that have never valued me properly. I got you, sis.

And finally to our Relentless Church family. Pastor Av and I love you all so much! This journey has been amazing, scary, filled with miracles, and so much more. And just think, this is only the beginning! My prayer for you as a church is that you will have victory in every area of your life—starting from the inside out. Let's win. From within.

About the Author

John W. Gray III is the senior pastor of Relentless Church in Greenville, South Carolina, and continues to serve as an associate pastor of America's largest single-venue church, Lakewood Church, in Houston, Texas. He preaches primarily at Lakewood's midweek service, where thousands converge each week. John was named to Oprah's SuperSoul 100, a collection of a hundred awakened leaders who are using their voices and talent to elevate humanity. His show, *The Book of John Gray*, airs on the Oprah Winfrey Network. John resides in Greenville with his wife, Aventer, and their children, John W. Gray IV and Theory Aspyn-Sky Gray.